IT Organization

ISBN 0-13-022298-4

9 780130 222985

HARRIS KERN'S ENTERPRISE COMPUTING INSTITUTE

HARRIS KERN'S ENTERPRISE COMPUTING INSTITUTE

IT
Organization

Building a Worldclass Infrastructure

Harris Kern
Stuart Galup
Guy Nemiro

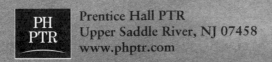

Prentice Hall PTR
Upper Saddle River, NJ 07458
www.phptr.com

Editorial/production supervision: *Vincent Janoski*
Acquisitions editor: *Greg Doench*
Marketing manager: *Miles Williams*
Manufacturing manager: *Alexis Heydt*
Cover design director:*Jerry Votta*
Series design: *Gail Cocker-Bogusz*

Published by Prentice Hall PTR
Prentice-Hall, Inc.
Upper Saddle River, NJ 07458

Printed in the United States of America
10 9 8 7 6 5 4 3 2 1

ISBN   0-13-022298-4

Prentice-Hall International (UK) Limited, *London*
Prentice-Hall of Australia Pty. Limited, *Sydney*
Prentice-Hall Canada Inc., *Toronto*
Prentice-Hall Hispanoamericana, S.A., *Mexico*
Prentice-Hall of India Private Limited, *New Delhi*
Prentice-Hall of Japan, Inc., *Tokyo*
Prentice-Hall Asia Pte. Ltd.
Editora Prentice-Hall do Brasil, Ltda., *Rio de Janeiro*

Contents

Preface

Structure, Not Technology

This book brings an urgent message for any Information Technology professional who is responsible for planning, implementing, managing, and supporting client/server (or networked) computing environments. If you want to survive in the networked, client/server world, you must stop, analyze, reorganize and prioritize your infrastructure now.

We spent two years analyzing 40, cross industry Fortune 1000 companies. We were engaged to assist IT organizations in their quest for reliability, availability, and serviceability (RAS) with client/server environments. This book is based on these case studies.

We found that organizations everywhere have serious latent infrastructure issues. Too often IT managers deal only with the symptoms of their problems by blaming technology, the complexity, or the architecture of client/server environments. The fact is that all of these companies have infrastructure issues that inhibit their ability to have RAS in client/server environments.

All of the companies we analyzed are committed to client/server computing and the transformation to the new paradigm (i.e., any data, anywhere, anytime) which is becoming more prevalent every minute in

Internet time. IT organizations must get their acts together to support their business requirements, but the terrifying fact is that IT organizations aren't prepared for the onslaught of the networked world because of the organizational problems we highlight.

The first section highlights the issues and problems of networked computing we found in our travels around the world. This section highlights what not to do.

The second section tells you how to look at the past for answers to the problems in today's environments. This section also shows you how to build that elusive world-class infrastructure.

The third section deals with how to structure your IT organization for the twenty-first century and how to give it a competitive advantage in the "dot comming" world.

And last, but so very important, are the questions we are asked most frequently by IT professionals during our travels.

This book is different than any other book we've written and any other books in the marketplace on IT organization structures because of the 40 case studies. This book is about the non-technical issues that IT organizations need to address to succeed in a client/server environment. This book is about basics—how to structure an organization so that it works. Through case studies and recommendations, we'll show you how to set up procedures, policies, and metrics to make sure the organization is effective.

Dedication

This book is dedicated to Ken Moskowitz, Doug Taggart, and Steve Levy from the Standard & Poor's IT organization. Ken is the CIO, Steve is Executive Vice President for Applications Development, and Doug is the Executive Vice President of Infrastructure. These gentlemen have created an atmosphere at S&P that's second to none. In the five years we've been visiting with IT organizations around the world we have been looking for an IT environment that's willing to apply our methodologies to build that elusive world-class infrastructure. Well, we found one, and it's theirs at S&P.

Most of our time was spent with Doug's organization. His direct reports are Stephanie Jason, Manager of the Help Desk; Rich Adams,

Director of Global Technologies; John Andrews, Director of Network Operations; and Nikki Gomez, Director of Client Services.

Not only was it a pleasure to work with these people, but they understood the vision, methodologies, and what it truly takes to implement a world-class infrastructure. They've created an organizational structure that supports people, processes and technology.

Acknowledgments

From Harris Kern: My congratulations to Paul Zazzera, the CIO at Time, Inc., and his staff. When we first visited their IT shop 1995 to perform an infrastructure assessment, it was one of the worst-run environments we had ever seen. We visited them once again in 1999 to see if things had improved. Today they are in the top five of the world's most cost-efficient IT organizations.

To Michael Hawkins for his friendship and contributions on the New Enterprise series and the Enterprise Computing Institute. Michael's enthusiasm, support, and knowledge have been one of the primary reasons that both have been successful.

Thanks to Steve McKenna for his support and friendship. Steve truly understands the importance of having a reliable, available, and serviceable IT infrastructure.

I would also like to thank my wife, Hanny, for her special love and support. Without her great cooking I would never be able to remain healthy and work the number of hours that I do.

From Stuart Galup: I would like to thank Harris Kern for his friendship. He is a great writing partner and a knowledgeable information technology professional. I wish him luck with his series and hope to have the pleasure of working with him on another book in the future.

I would also like to thank my wife, Dawn, and daughter, Christen, for their support.

From Guy Nemiro: I, too, thank Harris Kern for the education, support, and leadership he has shown me. I'm grateful for the helpful insights from Al Fortag, Dan Kronstadt, Rich Schiesser, Terry Tolman, Craig Williams, and John Wingler.

Introduction

We've traveled the world during the past few years, assessing infrastructures for Information Technology (IT) organizations for Fortune 1000 companies and new upstarts that have become the major portals to the Internet with market caps worth billions. We found that all of the organizations studied were facing the pressures of global competition and were trying to accomplish more with fewer resources. We met with executives, managers, and technical staff in a variety of industries on five continents. They knew that their computing environments would not stand the test of time. They were searching for information technology solutions to help them achieve competitive advantage. We were hired to help them get ready for the next business millennium.

Most of the organizations implemented their infrastructures over ten years ago, in some cases they actually started 30 years ago. We found large installed bases of legacy and client/server application software. In many cases, these organizations had architectures that resembled a collage of software languages, data storage (e.g., flat files, RDBMS, etc.), hardware, networks, and you name it. In some cases it was downright scary what we found.

Yet, you might ask what's so wrong with something that has worked for over ten years. Ironically, in many cases there really wasn't anything wrong with the infrastructure from a technical point of view. It worked! It may have been messy, but it worked.

The fascinating common thread we found in these organizations was that they were asking for help to solve technical issues and we found non-technical problems. The majority of the organizations were doing a fair job with the technology. Their problems centered on people and process issues. Even the new Internet and electronic-commerce-based companies have the same problems in spite of the fact that they are brand new companies with brand new technologies.

The process for gathering the data to write this book is a story in itself. While the individual case-study stories would make for entertaining reading, it's the lessons that we highlight from our research that are important. In a way, this is like therapy for IT organizations. The good thing about dealing with organizations is that we can diagnose what doesn't work and prescribe what can. So, let's start at the beginning. There's really only one way to gather infrastructure-related data and that's to perform an audit or assessment of the computing environment.

The challenge for us when we visit an organization is to do our assessment in less than five days. Most big consulting firms typically require a minimum of 30 days to provide this type of service for Fortune 500 IT infrastructures. And, these surveys are usually accompanied by a hefty price. Don't get us wrong, there's nothing wrong with these 30-day assessments. The results are usually a lengthy, well-written, and very detailed document of over 100 pages, depicting the many infrastructure-related issues. Actually, these reports represent an overwhelming and disheartening list of issues.

The first time the CIO sees the document, he or she is very pleased at the level of detail and is full of enthusiasm to get started to resolve the numerous problems. A special staff meeting is called to order. In attendance are his or her direct reports. The main agenda item is discussed with action items assigned. From this point forward, things have a way of deteriorating or just collapsing for many reasons:

- Lack of funding to implement the recommendations.
- Lack of time and resources to take on the numerous problems.
- Executive management leaves the company. The new regime wants to do things their way.
- Business issues/requirements take precedence.
- No established metrics to determine how the recommendations are to be implemented.

- The issues documented in the report are usually not much of a shock to the team of managers.

Our approach had to be radically different. When we do an assessment our goal is to provide a written analysis based on an evaluation of less than five days that:

- Keeps things simple by focusing on one of our key methodologies (as discussed in Chapter 7)—minimum yet sufficient.
- Provides no more than six recommendations that would have a significant impact on resolving the most critical issues and provide RAS to the infrastructure.
- Provides a list of key methodologies. These methodologies become part of the overall vision when designing and implementing a worldclass infrastructure.
- Highlights the issues in three categories: People, Process, and Technology.
- Is based on separate 30-minute interviews with 15 to 25 IT staff and management personnel. Additional interviews are conducted with two of IT's customers.
- Results in a written report of about 30 pages depending on the size of the company.

It's difficult for executives to believe that we can provide the information necessary to build a worldclass infrastructure in just a few days. After all, consulting firms have been doing infrastructure assessments for a quarter century. The duration has almost always been 30 days.

It's doable in much less time and we proved it. If you've ever read any of our previous books, *Rightsizing the New Enterprise, Managing the New Enterprise, Networking the New Enterprise,* and *Building the New Enterprise*, you know we focus on streamlining and reengineering just about every aspect of the infrastructure. Every aspect of the IT infrastructure these days needs to be continuously scrutinized to see if it's a candidate for reengineering, and that includes the way we assess infrastructures.

IT Infrastructure Assessment

The IT infrastructure assessment is a one- to two-day review of an information systems organization. These assessments take a high-level snapshot of IT initiatives and issues within the infrastructure. We meet with key IT personnel, management and technicians, and key business personnel. The process is to have 30-minute interviews with mid-level IT management, senior executives, and—most important—the technical staff. We say that because technicians (in most companies) have a better understanding of the infrastructure and associated issues than management. And, just as important during the interview process, technicians don't have any hidden agendas. Managers too often have territorial and political conflicts.

We do interviews to understand the issues. The result is a report of about 30 pages providing recommendations on resolving those issues. The report is then presented to executive management with senior management usually present. Discussions are usually lively and very interactive. We've had 100 percent buy-in to date. Executive management buy-in is extremely important to the process. Without buy-in, the process is dead in its tracks. A copy of the assessment is included in Appendix A.

The rest of this book is based on the findings from these assessments and our experiences in solving these issues.

If you're wondering whether there's a template for the types of questions used in these 30-minute interviews, there really isn't. We start each interview by asking one question. From there it could go in dozens of different directions. It's pretty much something we have learned to do following our gut instinct. That one question goes something like this: "If you were to look at the people, processes, and technology issues here at your company, what would you say works and doesn't work in each of these categories?" We'll provide examples of what falls under the "people, process, and technology" categories (see Table 1–1). This is really a simple way to get to the heart of the matter and find one version of the truth. Nothing fancy, but it gets the ball rolling.

Our objective is to address the critical issues facing all IT managers today:

- Balancing technology issues with customer service.
- Promoting effective communications.
- Organizing to support the new enterprise.
- Dealing with cultural differences between legacy and client/server personnel.
- Defining support roles and responsibilities.

- Implementing performance metrics.
- Ensuring security.
- Reengineering IT processes.
- Managing change.
- Selecting and fully implementing System Management tools.
- Recruiting, retaining, and mentoring staff.
- Productionalizing client/server applications with RAS.
- Dealing with scarce resources to accommodate the variety of technologies.

What Is the Infrastructure?

We refer to the infrastructure as the network, data center facilities, server rooms, wiring, desktop, RDBMS, OS, integration, applications support, processes, metrics, service level agreements, systems management tools, all computer-related hardware, COTS (commercial off the shelf) software such as financial applications, e-mail systems office tools, and people. The most important ingredient and most difficult challenge is the staffing, the people, the human element. It's really everything to do with the computing environment.

Table 1–1

People	Processes	Technology
Organization structure	Change control	Hardware
Skills development	Metrics	Architectures
Roles and responsibilities	Problem management	Software
Cultural; Legacy Vs. Client/ Server mentalities	Disaster recovery	Integration
Communication	Performance and tuning	OS
Training	Security	RDBMS
Transitioning3 staff	Capacity planning	Server consolidation
Job descriptions	Software distribution	High availability (hardware)

Table 1–1

People	Processes	Technology
Career path	Asset management	System management tools
Retaining staff	Event monitoring	Applications development tools
Mentoring staff	Network management	Standards
	System management tools	Data warehouse
	Production acceptance	
	QA	
	Storage management	
	Scheduling	
	Service level agreements	
	Benchmark services	
	Charge-back	
	Version/Release management	
	Service level agreements	

There's one area of the infrastructure with which we purposely are only dealing in a partial way: applications or systems development.

This area is flourishing more than ever before. After all, this is the area everyone has been focusing on throughout the 1990s. In the 1960s, 1970s, and early 1980s, applications development took a back seat to the infrastructure. Now the roles are reversed. In our opinion—based on the studies we performed—applications development is not the problem except that the process of developing applications must take into account how the applications or systems will be supported in the production environment. We've seen too many instances where the development staff has created applications in a vacuum without regard to how they will be used in the production world. When this happens, the applications development team can't meet with success because the applications can't successfully go live.

The issues the applications developers have (i.e., development tools, processes, QA, etc.) are not as severe as the production support side of the infrastructure. For the purposes of this book we'll exclude applications development when we refer to the infrastructure and that's only because the problems are not as serious in this area. The issues the applications developers have are not as severe as the production support side of the infrastructure.

This all started in the late eighties when client/server gained enormous popularity. IT's customers just wanted to build new systems as quickly as possible. They could not have cared less about the infrastructure. Maybe that's a bit harsh. It's not that they didn't care, it's that there was never the time or budget to address it properly. Herein lies the problem. This has been going on for over a decade now. Starting in the sixties, it took over two decades to get the mainframe infrastructure to where it is today: a highly reliable, available, and serviceable (RAS), yet bureaucratic computing environment. In the past 10+ years we've been incorporating new technologies (e.g., Unix and NT) in this environment at a torrid pace without investing in resolving people and process issues to compensate for this influx of technology. You cannot keep pushing and pushing without focusing on the people and process issues. The infrastructure is bleeding profusely, and IT management had better start paying attention.

What We Found in Our Travels

Since our first book was published in 1994, we've worked with companies all over the world, presenting at large functions, and teaching classes on the subject of how to effectively implement and manage client/server infrastructures. We provided insight on how to deal with the people and process issues. The reception and feedback were very positive. Since 1994 we've published four additional books on this same subject. Sales figures were excellent so we assumed the interest was still there, but why aren't all these infrastructure-related problems with client/server computing being addressed?

In our travels we learned a heck of a lot in visiting with more than 500 companies (probably closer to 1,000). The most apparent issue is how inefficiently client/server environments are being run. But that's putting it mildly. It's been getting worse year after year, and what's so disheartening is that there is very little to look forward to in the next several years.

These corporations are having a terrible time attaining RAS. No wonder metrics weren't being kept on server availability. How embarrassing it is to show that your servers were up 70 to 80 percent of the time. The customers were complaining about the hardware and their vendor without stepping back to look and see if their house (infrastructure) was in order.

In this section we document the problems from data gathered from more than 40 case studies and share the bad news with you.

What's Wrong with Client/Server?

The problems are enormous! Client/server computing is flying by the seat of its pants. There's no planning. There are no metrics. Roles and responsibilities are not clearly defined. There are very few processes that are implemented, maintained, and monitored. Communication within Information Technology and with IT's customers is worse than ever before. It's a real mess out there. But this is only the beginning.

It's no shock to IT professionals that there are problems with client/server computing but what's eye opening are the number and severity of the problems. We traveled the world in search of a well run client/server-computing environment with RAS to benchmark. And we searched and searched. We searched for over two years and we came up dry. What in the world is going on here? We needed to find the answers.

Our data was compiled from performing one- to two-day IT infrastructure assessments. We ended up performing more than 40 of these assessments with major corporations around the world. The results were disheartening and difficult to fathom.

The Problems

Table 2–1 points out the most common problems and their overall impact on the infrastructure.

Table 2–1   Properties of Fact and Dimension

Problem	Impact
Many IT shops are organizing to focus on particular technologies (i.e. Mainframe, AS400, NT, Unix, Novel, etc.).	• Poor communication among groups. • Duplication of System Management efforts. • Poor morale. • Lack of enterprise-wide solutions. • Huge walls between the groups. • Limited technical resources.
Some infrastructure organizations structure to focus on high-visibility projects and have a separate structure to focus on production support.	• Difficult to turn over projects from development to support. • Poor morale. • Technicians would prefer to work on new projects rather than be labeled as full-time, production-support personnel

Table 2–1   Properties of Fact and Dimension

Problem	Impact
The Architecture function has proven to be ineffective for designing infrastructures. The CIO might think otherwise because one of the architect's functions is to help design the proper infrastructure. It may be their function but we have yet to see this work effectively.	• Infrastructure development lags further behind the needs of the customers and IT.
Lack of a production control function (production Q/A, second-level system administration, process ownership, etc.).	• There's only one level of support for System Administration functions — all problems go directly to senior technical staff. • Lack of junior system administrator skill development. • systems management tools not fully implemented, customized, and maintained. Not enough time to do the job right. • Senior technical staff cannot properly plan and design the infrastructure because they're too busy firefighting problems.
Duplication of system management efforts. In many instances staff is only looking at point solutions to address the issues to support the technology for which they are responsible.	• Wasted technical resource cycles. • Higher costs to IT. • Lack of enterprise-wide solutions. • Fingerpointing among groups.
Lack of skilled resources. Most IT shops we visited are not taking the time to breed technical expertise within the organization. They're only looking at external recruitment efforts.	• The competition is fierce in the marketplace. Most of the companies we visited with are putting all their energy into external recruiting. This leaves a big void—they need to start breeding within the organization as well as continue to look at external resources.
Retaining senior technical staff is difficult. In all the environments we visited the technical staff is in a constant firefighting/reactive mode.	• Frustration of staff because of chaotic state of the infrastructure. • Career development is limited to solving day-to-day problems. • Burnout is imminent.
Lack of junior technical staff career development. The organization doesn't promote the proper career path.	• Management can only recruit technical staff from limited external sources. • Lack of skilled technical resources.

Table 2–1 Properties of Fact and Dimension

Problem	Impact
Job functions overlapping. Roles and responsibilities are not clearly defined.	• Duplication of efforts. • Confusion in the ranks for problem resolution, especially for the Help Desk staff as they're tasked to resolve problems as quickly as possible. • Problem management is difficult to define and administer. • Staff is responsible for many things but very few own any of it. • Production support confusion reigns throughout IT.
Communication is extremely poor.	• Wasted efforts. • Inefficient use of resources. • Projects take more time, resources, and money to implement. • Service levels difficult to maintain. • Users frustrated with IT.
Problem management is ineffective.	• High availability becomes an unattainable goal. • Lack of problem ownership. • People are tied up in priorities—they don't have the time to document the problems/issues. • Lack of follow-up. • Problems get lost—no tracking. • There's a lack of information. • Lack of root cause analysis. • Lack of closed-loop feedback. • Level 2 analysts not putting in detailed description of how they resolved the problem. • Many of the groups provide no feedback on problems being worked.
Multiple Help Desks.	• Confusion for end-users. • Duplication of efforts. • Multiple owners — or no ownership — of a very critical problem management process. • Higher costs.
Lack of effective processes.	• RAS unattainable.

Table 2–1 Properties of Fact and Dimension

Problem	Impact
Help Desk improperly structured within the organization.	● Lack of authority.
LAN support is split among multiple organizations.	● Confusion for end-users. ● Duplication of efforts. ● Higher costs to IT.
Database administration not centralized; in many companies it's organized under applications development, for others in operations support, and for others it's split between the two.	● Causes poor communication. ● Problem resolution not as effective. ● Duplication of efforts. ● Not equal emphasis on analysis and administration
Some IT shops are splitting the infrastructure group between infrastructure development and production support.	● Poor communication. ● Poor morale. ● Duplication of efforts. ● Turf battles.
System management tools are not fully implemented.	● Manual intervention. ● Wasted costs. ● Occasional glitches. ● Wasted technical resources.
Lack of a tape librarian function.	● Integrity compromised. ● Minimum disaster recovery requirements are nonexistent.
Global coordination is not effective.	● Poor communication. ● Frustration. ● Duplication of efforts.
Lack of an effective change control process.	● RAS compromised.
Lack of a client/server application production acceptance process.	● No production QA function. ● Poor communication between IT and its customers. ● Production support and applications development are not communicating early on in the application deployment cycle.
Lack of metrics.	● Cannot effectively manage the infrastructure unless you know the numbers.

Table 2–1 Properties of Fact and Dimension

Problem	Impact
Lack of an effective curriculum to effectively transition the legacy staff.	• Limited technical resources. • Poor morale. • Wasted IT costs.
Lack of a strategic process to market and sell IT services. IT needs to communicate its services with its customers.	• Poor relations with customers. • Users don't know where to turn for services
Lack of service levels.	• Expectations not properly documented between end-users and IT.
Lack of a process to benchmark services.	• Management can continue threatening to outsource IT.
Not measuring customer satisfaction	• Disastrous
Lack of data center mentoring.	• Moving forward to effectively support mission critical client/server applications regardless of the platform and paradigm is extremely difficult. It is critical to take the best practices from the legacy environment and the most important methodologies from open systems to come up with the best of both worlds.
Complexity in the organization structure.	•Ineffective use of resources. •Poor communication. •Duplication of efforts.
Lack of standards and lack of adherence to standards throughout the enterprise	•Duplication of efforts. •Poor communication. •Higher costs. •Wasted technical resources.

There are so many problems with today's infrastructure. The top problems (in no particular order except the first) in today's client/server environments, based on the 40 assessments are:

1. The organization structure

2. Lack of an enterprise-wide change management process

3. Lack of an effective problem management process

4. Lack of a production acceptance process

5. Lack of metrics
6. Lack of a proper curriculum to transition/mentor staff
7. Communication is worse than ever before
8. Not fully implementing system management tools
9. Lack of senior technical resources
10. Lack of a process to market/sell and benchmark IT services
11. Lack of service levels between operational support and applications development and also between IT and its customers
12. Recruiting/retaining technical resources

These aren't surprising to IT professionals. But what is astonishing is that the No. 1 problem is the organization structure for each and every company we visited. This is incredible!

After the first half dozen assessments, we realized that client/server computing was making a mockery of the IT profession because many of the problems pointed back to the organization. Each one of these assessments highlighted major problems with the way the organization was structured. How can that be? Structuring the organization to support a new paradigm couldn't be that difficult. It isn't, but the biggest problem is that IT executives know that client/server computing is so much more complex. So they try to overcompensate by focusing on particular technologies or high-visibility projects.

Reorganizations are occurring at a torrid pace, like never before. Most of the companies we visited reorganized at a minimum of every six months. In the legacy days, once a year was a big-news event. But we can't blame all these intelligent executives. Something needs to be done to introduce RAS into these chaotic networked computing environments.

So why is network computing so difficult to get our arms around? Very few understand where the problems really are. With so much talk of technology these days, many IT professionals look at technology as their savior, the more the better to solve these problems. They gobble it up and plop it down. It seems logical. So why isn't it working? Why can't companies attain a high-level of RAS as we have on the mainframe? The technology everyone's gobbling up is definitely mature enough to manage a mission critical production environment.

Legacy-minded critics blame client/server computing. This is ridiculous. For decades we focused all energy on people and process issues to have an environment that is reliable, available, and serviceable. RAS starts with the organization.

This is not rocket science. Yet, why is it so difficult to structure the organization to accommodate RAS when we have all these highly educated and experienced IT professionals? Executives have used every excuse in the book to reorganize.

The Excuses

- The business is changing.
- We have some hot new technology requiring resources.
- Our company is downsizing; we need to restructure.
- We have to separate the legacy environment from the other stuff because we want to sustain RAS.

The real issue is client/server computing. It is like nothing IT veterans or, for that matter, younger executives have ever come across. Yet they're not admitting it. How do you structure for something that has no boundaries or clear demarcations? We'll show you throughout this book.

What made us so smart? Why did we find the answers? Two reasons. First, our backgrounds helped. We were reared in a legacy mission-critical data center environment. We were also chartered with transitioning large legacy computing environments to client/server. Second, we have no biases. There is such an ugly perception that managers of legacy computing environments are bureaucratic, maintain costly environments, and are behind the times, etc. Sure, a lot of that is true, but what about RAS? What about when you came to work and the systems were always up and running? That's where mission-critical, high-availability evolved. All we ask people to do as they read the book is to look at what worked and what didn't work in the legacy environment to effectively move forward.

Applications Development Is Not an Issue

Why did we pick on the infrastructure group and say nothing about applications development? Surely applications development can't be perfect. It's not, but the issues are small compared to the infrastructure group. In the late eighties and throughout the nineties the focus was to develop and deploy quickly. The infrastructure took the backseat. In the seventies the Infrastructure drove the car and owned the back seat—applications development was somewhere in the trunk. Times have changed. You need both groups playing together to be successful. Without the proper infrastructure there cannot be RAS when deploying new systems, and when the systems cannot maintain high availability, all of IT gets a black eye.

The Impact

There is, however, an impact from the infrastructure group that hits applications development right where it counts — rolling out new production-quality systems. When deploying new systems there needs to be a process that ensures quality assurance (QA), that promotes and instills effective communication practices between applications development and production support. There needs to be a checklist to engage key personnel from the beginning. This same checklist needs to ensure adherence to disciplines (i.e., change control). There is such a process, which we refer to as the Client/Server Production Acceptance (CSPA). Please read Chapter 7 in our book *Building the New Enterprise* or Chapter 9 in our book *Managing the New Enterprise*.

The two groups need to work together when deploying new systems. applications development needs production support, and production support has a responsibility to service applications development.

Processes Are Not First

Organizing to support RAS should be first. Structure the organization properly to support a mission-critical environment. Don't reorganize because you're implementing a new process. Many shops do this, but it's wrong. Once you restructure to support RAS, the organization will have clearly-defined process ownership. Processes need one owner for design, implementation, and maintenance.

The CIO's Role

In this section we discuss the CIO's role as we enter the 21st century. Executives will have little choice but to start focusing at least 50 percent of their time to getting their house (infrastructure) in order. This is due to global competition, business requirements/issues, shrinking IT budgets, and unhappy customers. They will have no choice but to get involved. It's not too late.

How times have changed. The MIS managers in the 1970s and 1980s knew every aspect of their infrastructure. There were no surprises. They were very much in tune with their infrastructure, especially those people and process issues we discuss throughout the book. They let their system programmers and DBAs worry about the technology. Their biggest concern was RAS. The MIS managers of yesteryear were the ones responsible for providing us with high reliability, availability, and serviceability. IT wouldn't be what it is today without their relentless pursuit of RAS. We can learn from their experiences and the way they managed. They were involved, they spent time in the trenches with the enlisted. They knew exactly what was being done. They were credible leaders to their troops because they typically came up from the ranks and had established their expertise.

Today is a whole new ballgame. Yet, to be successful, they need to show the same leadership as their peers of the 1970s, and they need to set accountability standards.

Infrastructures are bending, bleeding, and becoming more costly than ever because everyone's supporting more disparate systems than ever before. Very little time is being focused on implementing key processes. Actually, the organization structure is so far off center that processes would not be effective in this environment.

CIOs everywhere have been focusing on new systems development and deployment because that's how they've been getting rewarded by their bosses and other peers in the executive ranks who believe that development is where they get the biggest bang for the buck. After all, it is the politically correct thing to do. The quicker new systems are deployed to meet the needs of the business, the easier it is for the CIO to gain peer respect in the short run. Unfortunately, the modus operandi does not encourage long-term planning.

What about the long-term impacts of continuously adding client/server information systems? If the new applications don't fit into the overall IT architecture, or don't have ample bandwidth or adequate support from the DBAs, they don't work. Believe us, we've seen too many examples of well-intended projects going amok because they were created in vacuums without consideration to the infrastructure required to support them.

Executives Out of Touch with Their Infrastructure

Executive management needs to get involved! Things are desperately out of control with the IT infrastructure. Yet they don't really know how bad it is. It's a real mess out there as depicted in Table 3–1. The problem is that executive management is overloaded and now it's become a crisis.

As a first step, management needs to dedicate one solid week to gaining an understanding of the issues their organization is facing. Just one week in the trenches with the technical staff! Executives need to spend the time with their technical staff, not management, to get the true picture. The horrors they uncover will shock them. A wakeup call that they'll never forget. This is a necessity!

But that's not enough. Executive management can establish a set of common metrics to judge how well the organization is meeting its daily, short-term and long-term objectives. By having common metrics, everyone in the organization will speak the same lingo. Think about the data centers of the 1960s and 1970s. Typically, the data center was one location where everyone worked together. Compare that to today where the applications development staffs are scattered around the world, the data center has become a compendium of different data centers, and executives are not located together. It's no wonder that people are out of touch with one another—and why executives are so easily out of touch with their organizations. The point is for everyone to be in touch with what's happening, to have up-to-the minute news and measurements for performance so that management can be active, not reactive.

With a common set of metrics that everyone in the organization understands, everyone on the IT team can immediately gauge how the team is doing against its own measurements. Our contention is that you achieve high-level RAS only when you understand what the measurements mean. Too often we've seen IT executives gloss over the nuts and bolts of making RAS possible. We've seen executives assume that RAS is the responsibility of lower level data center and network managers, without understanding the linkage of the different components that make this possible. By having a common metric system for RAS, different managers can see how different departments are performing and they can correlate results among departments.

Supporting client/server applications encompasses multiple hardware and software components that must be monitored to ensure a RAS environment. Products such as Hewlett-Packard's OpenView and Computer Associates' UniCenter can provide seamless interfaces to hardware and software products to gather operational statistics and other data. Microsoft's MSM and Paradigm's desktop software management tools can provide for desktop management and ensure that only approved software is loaded on desktops.

Information about the network computing environment is critical for RAS. The dashboard of information should include basic data points such as:

- Assets inventory (network-wide hardware and software)
- Network connection(s)
- Network performance (including data packet management)
- Desktop software (inventory control)
- Database(s) connections

- Database(s) availability (session status)

- Database(s) performance

- Operating system(s) availability

- Operating system(s) performance

How Can the Infrastructure Catch Up Quickly?

This is the $64,000 question. The answer is that the infrastructure can't catch up very easily. It takes time and resources. You tell us who in the world of IT has that luxury today? Not too many organizations, but the alternative is to let client/server die a slow death. Everywhere we go management is complaining to anyone who will listen. The poor vendors providing client/server solutions are feeling the brunt of it. The complaints are the same in every part of the world—client/server is not as reliable, available, and serviceable as the mainframe world. We've heard this for almost ten years now. You know what? They're right, and we might also add that on a scale of one to ten, if the mainframe infrastructure was an eight (it had some major flaws), then client/server has to be a two (and that's being generous). Ten years later, and only a two. How pathetic.

You know IBM is sitting back and enjoying this. IBM is telling customers that the mainframe didn't have these RAS issues. And, IBM isn't alone. The Unix vendors, such as Sun, HP and even IBM are bringing to market massively powerful, multi-domain servers which are designed to serve a similar purpose as mainframes, namely to host a variety of applications on the same box. Even so, with n-tier or client/server computing, the fact remains that computing in the next millennium will be more intricate and more network-based which means that the people and process issues are glaring and still with us.

There is hope. Start small. Don't try to take on everything at once. The issues are enormous. Determine what the top three to five problems are within your IT computing environments by doing a high-level assessment, and follow the steps in Chapter 8 on what it takes to build a world-class infrastructure. Then, set up a measurement system to track how well the organization is performing.

Lack of Time and Resource

There is a severe lack of time and resource to build the proper infrastructure. Many of the issues we've highlighted have already been identified. They are on that infamous list of goals year in and year out. These issues have been on the back burner for too long. New technology or new systems continue to take precedence. It's the same story no matter where we go. The pendulum will never shift back to the way we built infrastructures in the 1970s and 1980s when the infrastructure was priority number one and everything else was a lesser priority. However, the proportion of 90 percent applications development and 10 percent infrastructure development will be the death of client/server computing because the system will fail, and so will its leaders.

If you heard from the CIOs we listened to, you would hear their argument that on the one side they have a Vice President of Applications Development and on the other side they have a VP of Infrastructure or Operations, both with large budgets and extensive staffs. They claimed that because of their organization's large staff and budget for infrastructure, they spent nearly half their time on operations. But, they also admitted that they focused most of their energies on applications development, not really understanding the issues with their infrastructure. It's a matter of focus. Until CIOs concentrate on improving the structure of their organization, they won't have RAS with networked client/server computing.

So, the role of the CIO is to harness the available resources, decide what projects can be undertaken to succeed, and set up a viable measurement system so that the organization knows how it's performing on daily, mid-range, and long-range basis.

Assure That Your IT Budget Provides for RAS

As the leader of the IT organization, it's up to the CIO to make sure that the budget has ample production support services to attain RAS. Many application promotions become disasters because they are created without regard for budget costs and the additional overhead for production services.

Many costs are incremental and are, therefore, not full costs. They must be budgeted as full costs. For example, the addition of an application to the production portfolio may only add a workload equal to a half-time equivalent persons in the database administration support group. Unfortunately, unless the organization has an arrangement with a part-time DBA service provider, the cost of support will grow to one FTE or the existing staff will be faced with the added burden without increased personnel. In some cases this may be handled for a budget cycle with overtime dollars, but it is not recommended.

The CIO must oversee the budget cycle or delegate this responsibility to someone in the organization. Either way, you want to make sure that the budget checklist includes:

1. Database administration (user database management, DBMS administration, monitoring, and performance tuning).

2. Server administration (operating system administration, monitoring and performance tuning).

3. Network administration (network administration, monitoring and performance tuning).

4. Data center operations (backups, recovery, monitoring, and disk management).

5. Personnel costs related to database administration, server administration, network administration, and data center operations.

6. Hardware, software licensee and upgrade costs. These items may be required for development, QA, and production systems.

7. Supplies such as paper, disks, tapes, manuals, and printing costs.

8. Training costs, especially flexibility in calendar assignments so that staff can attend classes.

9. Help-desk support.

10. Additional or upgraded license fees to support new or enlarged applications.

11. Maintenance contracts from hardware and software vendors.

12. Facilities and utilities.

Marketing and Selling IT Services

This still isn't being done. We've been talking about this concept since the early nineties but we have yet to see much progress. This needs to be a full time job function. Not a separate function, but as part of each and every manager's responsibility. Once again, we know that no one has the time, but this cannot be an excuse any longer. As the leader of IT, the CIO must take responsibility to market IT's services and mission throughout the company.

IT still has a rotten image out there and client-server computing has made things worse. "IT is spending millions and what are we getting in return?" is the most common theme. Now, we ITers know better—customers are getting plenty of service but they still complain and say they receive very little attention from IT. This perception has to go away once and for all.

Let's face it, in the era of outsourcing, any IT organization is in competition with other providers that might provide this service better, cheaper, and more efficiently to the enterprise.

Today, IT professionals need to start by thoroughly documenting their services with associated costs for those services. They need to walk with the great unwashed and communicate with customers. Schmooze, sell, and otherwise promote your services. Examples of ways IT can promote its services and value are located in Appendix D.

Table 3–1   Internal marketing examples

Activity	Description
Newsletters	Publish a quarterly newsletter to be distributed to your primary customers in the organization outlining your recent successes, updates to your business plan, and plans for the near- and long-term future. Include statistics showing improvements in supporting customers, such as: ● Uptime availability of the network. ● Uptime of applications. ● Savings business units enjoy as a result of applications that have been deployed to support in-line business units. ● Number of help-desk queries handled in a fiscal quarter.

Table 3–1   Internal marketing examples

Activity	Description
Assign IT representatives to be liaisons with business unit executives, and coordinate regularly scheduled meetings with the business units.	The CIO and representatives to business units meet with the internal customers to review their business relationships.
Tours of the data center	Host periodic tours to acquaint your customers with your facilities and the staff.
Implement an internal IT homepage.	Publish information about your IT organization, its mission, services, organizational structure, and accomplishments.

Duplication of Efforts

Although many of these corporations have legitimate staff shortages, there is also duplication of efforts throughout the organizations as highlighted by the issues in Table 2–1 in Chapter 2. When performing these assessments, management will often ask if the final report will recommend additional headcount. Our answer is that only 30 percent of the companies we studied had a real manpower deficiency. Rarely (maybe 10 percent of the time) do we recommend additional resources because of the many problems with these networked infrastructures. Adding headcount to these types of environments will only make senior management look bad because the problems will not go away by just adding resources.

So, how can the CIO determine if there's duplication of efforts? The answer lies in thoroughly understanding the organization and the different operational groups and their inter-related functions. The one-week analysis will give top management an opportunity to analyze the organization and see where overlap occurs, and where there are gaping holes in the support of RAS. The follow-on creation of metrics measurement will help everyone understand how to judge the performance of RAS and its importance to achieving IT's mission.

Outsourcing Is Not Necessarily the Quick Fix

The average tenure for a CIO is about 2 years. This will get worse in the future. Many new CIOs will inherit a disaster (one of these infrastructures). Their first reaction—and maybe the seemingly politically correct thing to do—will be to investigate how to outsource this mess.

CIOs, beware. If you outsource a mess, you'll get twice the headaches in return. Besides, we have yet to see an outsourcing vendor do a good job with client/server computing. What makes you think they can get it right? Like we said, 40 for 40 out there, and no one has gotten it right yet. They have some good salesmen that can promise the world. But words alone will not be the answer. If you're itching to outsource something, then let it be a well-run legacy environment, which any outsourcing vendor can effectively support.

Alternatively, selective outsourcing like the Help Desk or the Network will work. For additional information on outsourcing, please read our book *Building the New Enterprise*.

Case Studies

For years we've known of the issues with client/server computing as highlighted in Table 2–1. For years we've also been pleading with IT management all over the world to do something about these problems before it's too late. It's obvious we haven't succeeded in communicating the urgency of the problem. Let's give it one more try.

If IT management wouldn't listen to us before, we thought eyes might start opening if they saw case study data from 40 Fortune 1000-class companies. Sometimes it's easier to look objectively at someone else's organization to see the blatant problems . . . easier than looking at one's own problems.

These case studies are from companies spanning across different industries, including finance, manufacturing, media, transportation, retail, etc. We looked inside some of the largest, most established, and well-known companies in the world. We also looked at a few smaller yet fast growing companies, such as Internet service providers and other Internet-related companies.

Here we share the data that took almost two years to compile.

Our program to assess IT organizations was started because we knew of the ongoing frustrations and problems IT management was having in supporting client/server computing. We believed that, based on our experience of running client-server computing, we could provide valuable insights to others on how to manage their organizations. We have extensive experience running legacy and client-server shops.

Seventy-five percent of the companies we visited also had mainframe environments. What would any red-blooded IT professional do but compare RAS in the two environments? The results are not surprising. The mainframe would win hands down. Every organization reported better RAS statistics and experiences with the mainframe compared to client-server computing. It was the same in the US as in Asia or Europe, the same in manufacturing companies as at the movie studios as in aerospace firms. The simple truth is that no one has the same frustrations in the legacy world as in the client/server world.

Everywhere we've gone we've heard the same story, namely that the client/server environment isn't as stable, or as disciplined, or as secure as the older legacy environments. If we were CIOs from one of these 40 companies, we would say the same thing they did because they, like us, had success with RAS in their mainframe legacy environments of yesteryear. We've had success with RAS in legacy environments and with client/server computing. Thus, we were confident of our ability to consult and offer our vision and guidance.

But we all know that talk is easy. The actual building of an infrastructure with RAS takes many years to get it right. In the legacy environment we focused on the infrastructure first and it still took years. Do you remember who was directly involved with every aspect of developing a state-of-the-art infrastructure? You got it, the MIS manager who was the 1970s version of today's CIO. The MIS manager's office was near or next to the Data Center, that temple of RAS. There wasn't a day that went by that he or she didn't put on their white gloves and inspect the beautiful glass house. It was their showcase to the world. All visitors (even vendors) received a tour whether they asked for one or not. They had rules—rules that provided RAS—and rules that were a bit excessive. There better not be a speck of dust, waste in the garbage can, or a cable lying around where it shouldn't be, or heads would roll. Yet, metrics were abundant and accurate.

Let's get back to the case studies. Why did we wait until after 40 site evaluations to write about this? The proof is in these assessments. Forty for 40, they all depict major flaws in the organization structure. Table 4–1 points out these organizational-related problems and their impact. These problems are highlighted in the table to bring you visibility and awareness of the mess these computing environments are in today. Unreal, isn't it! If we were to see this for the first time we probably wouldn't believe it either. The same issues and problems over and

Table 4–1 Organizational Problems and Their Impact

Organizational Problems	Impact
Organizations today do not accommodate centralized ownership of key enterprise-wide processes (i.e., change control, problem management, etc.).	• Ineffective use of IT resources • Ineffective processes. • Sporadic application unavailability. • Loss of IT credibility with users. • RAS severely impacted. • Lack of enterprise-wide solutions. Groups have their own versions of these processes within IT.
Three levels of technical support (system administration) not defined.	• Problems go directly to senior technical staff. Senior technical staff is too busy with daily fire-fighting (problem resolution) drills. These senior technicians should be spending 80 percent of their time developing architectures, fully implementing and customizing systems management tools, and designing a cost-effective infrastructure.
Systems management tools not fully implemented by as much as 80 percent.	• Manual intervention. • Occasional glitches. • Wasted costs. • Wasted functionality and senior technical resources.
Organization is split between infrastructure development and production support.	• Difficult to turn over new projects developed within the infrastructure group to production support. • Difficult to designate a senior technician for production support only.
Organization does not intentionally and systematically breed senior technical staff.	• Technical resources scarce. • Senior technical staff bogged down with daily problem resolution. • Loss of opportunity to grow internal IT staff.
Lack of a production control function to support the client/server environment.	• Lack of production Q/A process. • Lack of second-level support. • Lack of centralized process ownership.

Table 4–1 Organizational Problems and Their Impact

Organizational Problems	Impact
Lack of an effective architecture/planning function.	• Cannot build an automated production-support environment • Lack of enterprise-wide solutions. • Lack of standards.
Lack of highly skilled technical resources especially in the systems administration function.	• Staff is in a continuous reactive mode without ample time to plan or architect a new infrastructure. Always too busy fire fighting. • Systems management tools not implemented properly.
Difficult for staff to keep abreast of technologies. Too busy with daily fire-fighting drills.	• Technology is evolving quicker than ever. System Management planning/analysis is imperative in implementing more of a lights-out environment. Thus, the organization loses out on opportunities to optimize use of new technologies.
Lack of enterprise-wide system management planning.	• Point vs. enterprise solutions. • Higher costs to IT. • Lack of enterprise-wide solutions.
Roles and responsibilities not clearly defined.	• Wasted human resource. • Duplication of efforts and overlap throughout the organization. • Wasted costs to IT. • Confusion for the people who use and staff the Help Desk. • Duplication of system management efforts.
In some companies we found organization structures to be extremely complex.	• Difficult to implement and administer processes. • Poor communication. • Problem management not effective.
Multiple groups supporting users. Sometimes there's a separate group responsible for desktop hardware and another for software. There's also a separate group responsible for desktop projects.	• At times difficult for the Help Desk to determine who to call for desktop problems. • Users lose time and productivity. • IT loses credibility.

Table 4–1 Organizational Problems and Their Impact

Organizational Problems	Impact
Everyone responsible for everything but rarely does someone own anything.	• Duplication of efforts throughout the organization. • Political infighting.
Some organizations are structured to focus on technology.	• Poor communication. • Poor morale. • Lack of enterprise-wide system management planning. • Resources become scarce.
Responsibilities overlap when splitting the infrastructure between development and support.	• Trying to separate projects and support is very difficult. Technical staff gets pulled off of support for new project implementations. Technicians prefer working on new projects. • Staff not implementing new projects has a difficult time supporting them. • Production support not receiving the recognition as does the staff working on new projects, but when problems occur they're the ones that work the overtime.

over again from company to company. Some have legacy environments and some don't. But what is apparent is that the infrastructure has truly taken a back seat to developing new systems. It's really a mess out there. Chances are executives wouldn't agree with us—they would never agree on something like that. They may change their minds when they see the data and the list of these 40 elite corporations. Then maybe they would start questioning their own IT computing environments.

The Problems Short-Listed

The problems are overwhelming, especially because so many of themare directly or indirectly affected by the organization structure. These were so incredible and mind-boggling that we decided to break up the problems into two sections, one for the organizational issues and one for everything else.

The primary reason for writing this book was to highlight the number of organizational-related issues. We wanted to bring even more focus to this subject; thus the impetus for breaking up all client/server problems into two sections. The severity and number of organizational-related issues were a big surprise to us and others with whom we discussed this subject. Without a doubt it is the biggest problem with client/server computing and deserves top billing.

Current Organizational Structures

This chapter shows the way many organizations are structured today. You wouldn't believe what we saw out there. Maybe you've seen the same setups, too. The first one (Figure 4–1) was our personal favorite and receives the first *DORG* (Disaster ORGanization) award. It's a designation that we give to organizations that have intrinsic problems just by the way they are created and the limitations they place on the people in the organization.

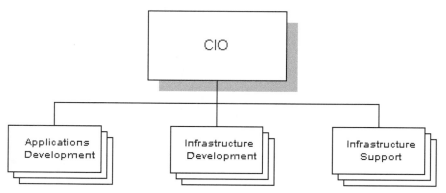

Figure 4–1 Infrastructure split in half.

The Infrastructure Split in Half.

In a few of the 40 companies we analyzed, we found the infrastructure was split between infrastructure development (implementing processes and technology) and infrastructure support (production support—full-time problem resolution). You can tell this idea came from someone in management whose career didn't evolve from the bowels of the data center or, for that matter, from someone who probably never headed up a large infrastructure group. If you've been in the industry and had the opportunity to know at least a handful of IT shops, you know that an increasing number of IT executives are appointed to their posts because top management thinks they have done well in other parts of the company. The net effect is that while IT requirements are growing dramatically, some IT executives lack the experience to really know how an IT organization works.

The structure had merit. They knew they had to focus on implementing processes and tools for their new client/server environment but they forgot about the biggest and most important part of the equation, the people aspect. If you were a technical person, would you like your role to be labeled production support or infrastructure development? We'll answer that one for you. All technical personnel would rather play with the latest widget and gadget than provide around-the-clock support. Playing with new technology is always more fun, so infrastructure development has more elan.

Splitting the infrastructure in half is by far the worst structure we've seen! It causes the following issues:

- Security privileges are shared. Security privileges should **never** be shared.
- Put yourself into the shoes of a senior technician. Why would anyone want to provide production support rather than test and implement the latest and greatest technology?
- Responsibilities overlap when splitting the organization.
- Difficult to turn over projects to support, especially since these projects were initiated and implemented in other organizations.
- Problem management becomes difficult—people will go to the expert for faster resolution.
- Duplication of system management efforts.
- Communication issues are worse than ever before.
- Cross-training constraints.
- Resource constraints.

There should be a happy medium. The answer is simple: Have just one infrastructure organization which is structured to provide three levels of technical support. This should be done for the Network, Desktop, and Data Center or Production Server room. Table 4–2 identifies three levels of support and the percentage of time required for each of the major functions.

We recommend that you have one infrastructure group.

Table 4–2 Three Levels of Support

Level of Support	Job Function	Percent
First	Monitoring/Problem resolution	80/20
Second	Problem resolution/Architecture development and technology analysis.	75/25
Third	Architecture development and technology analysis/ Problem resolution.	80/20

Focusing on Technology

In over half of the companies we visited, we found that IT organizations were divided to focus on technology, usually on the basis of operating systems. This is one of the most frequently used structures in the corporate world today. Another big-time DORG award. This structure is designed solely to focus on particular technologies. We usually see this structure in mainframe shops (see Figure 4–2).

The original intent was good. You need to start somewhere and heaven forbid if you corrupt your legacy environment with this crazy networked world. The big problem is after designing and implementing this structure, and after management says all the right words by telling the staff that one day the walls will come down, it rarely happens that way. The issues with structuring your organization in this manner are:

- Limitations on existing resources.
- Morale problems.
- Territorial boundaries.
- Cross-training constraints.
- Duplication of processes/tools.
- Extremely poor communication amongst the different groups.
- Lack of enterprise-wide systems management solutions.
- Limited skills development.

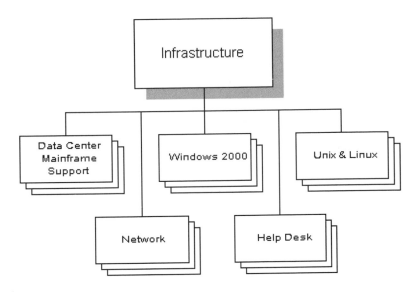

Figure 4–2 Organization structure focused on particular technologies.

We recommend these walls come down as quickly as possible. Start mentoring that a production system is a production system regardless of the box. This should be IT's mantra for the new millennium: A production system is a production system regardless of the box, application, or operating system.

The Architecture Function

The architecture function also deserves a DORG. At least 70 percent of the companies we've visited have this problem. Tell us, why didn't we need an architecture function back in the 1960s, 1970s, and early 1980s? Many argue that the infrastructure is so much more complex today than it was in the past. To some extent we will agree. Client/ server computing, as we said earlier, is like no other beast. But when we were mainframe computer operators or operations analysts, climbing the corporate ladder to become mainframe systems programmers, we viewed that world as a complex environment and it was. Assembler, TSO, VTAM, NCP, etc., created a complex information technology environment.

When we first started learning client/server, Unix, script programming, etc., it was difficult as well. Writing *Clists* was much more difficult than writing a shell script in Unix. It is all relative.

The architects in the mainframe era were systems programmers. The Systems Programmers of yesteryear built a darn good infrastructure because they were given the time to do so. There were three levels of support in the mainframe infrastructure:

- Level 1 — Operations and the Help Desk

- Level 2 — Production control (operations analyst)

- Level 3 — System programmer and database administrator

Rarely did systems programmers deal with daily problem resolution. In those days junior technicians (level one and two support personnel) were scared to death to disturb the mainframe gods. Everyone knew they were busy designing a temple. They were paid the big bucks to build an infrastructure that provided RAS, not to chase every problem that came into MIS. Think about it for a moment. It worked!

We have yet to see this function work effectively anywhere in the world. Why didn't the architecture function work when the concept sounded good? The function is supposed to:

- Keep abreast of technologies.

- Focus one set of eyes and ears to business requirements.

- Work with the infrastructure group to understand its needs.

- Provide guidance in establishing an architecture/roadmap.

We have yet to see it work as advertised. Do away with this function. Let your senior technical staff architect your infrastructure.

Database Administration

No DORG awards here. The database administration function is the most politically sensitive function for each of the large corporations we visited. We've seen the database administration group in three different areas of the organization. The first is within applications development as depicted in Figure 4–3. The second is within the infrastructure group as depicted in Figure 4–4. The third area is a mixture of both, as shown in Figure 4–5.

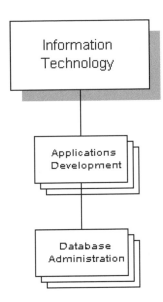

Figure 4–3   The database administration function within applications development.

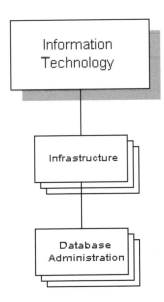

Figure 4–4   The database administration function within the infrastructure group.

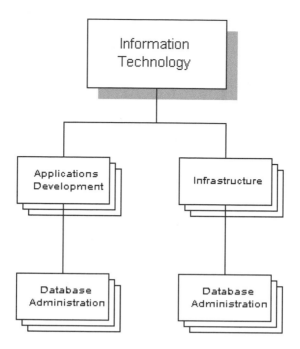

Figure 4–5   The database administration function within both applications development and the infrastructure group.

It's a tough call, but look back to our roots once again. In the mainframe world we centralized this function under the infrastructure group. The intention was to:

- Pool resources.
- Design enterprise-wide database administration solutions.
- Enhance career/skills development.
- Design and develop the architecture.
- Address performance and tuning issues.

So, help us out. What's wrong with that? One might argue that this group's focus should be on designing the proper database. If it's structured under the infrastructure group the perception would be that the database wouldn't be designed properly. We don't think that's realistic. Isn't the DBA function a service function just like any other function within IT? In the mainframe world the database group was centralized under the infrastructure group and things worked out just fine. As a matter of fact, our IDMS database in the eighties was extremely reliable. It couldn't have been designed any better, and that's because they wanted it perfect from the beginning so there would be fewer heartaches to deal with after it was in production.

We emphasize the recommendation that database administration should be centralized under the infrastructure group.

The Project Office

We just love giving out all these DORG awards. Once again the concept/theory gets some bonus points, but does it work? The project office was established to implement key processes like change control or applications development methodologies. When management conceived this organization their hearts were in the right place (see Figure 4–6). At least they knew that they needed to provide process design and implementation. Unfortunately, processes should only be designed and implemented by the folks in the trenches, not by people who are far removed from the front lines.

Back in the 1970s and 1980s we didn't need a special group to develop some of the most effective processes ever designed. What we had was a group we called production control which had centralized ownership of many of these critical processes. The processes themselves were developed by the Help Desk, Systems Programming, Database Administration, etc., and included:

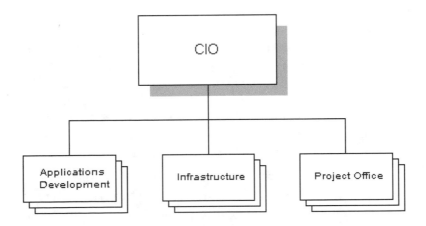

Figure 4–6   Structure designed to focus on process design.

- Problem management
- Change control
- Capacity planning
- Security

There's so much more, but we think you're getting the point.

Some of these groups are even responsible for disaster recovery. What's this world coming to? Once again, it's those senior technicians who should be in charge of disaster recovery. They'll figure out how to make this stuff work. Structure the organization properly and give them the bandwidth. Please don't take it out of their hands.

You're wasting company resources! Once again we didn't need it back in the mainframe days and don't tell us the environment was different than it is today. Sure it was, but the best processes (i.e., change control, problem management, etc.) were created in those days. Disaster Recovery was second to none. As we've circled the globe several times and visited with hundreds of Fortune 1000 companies, we have yet to see an effective disaster recovery solution for client/server computing, and not because the technology is so much more complex. It's been taken out of the hands of the senior gurus, those senior system administrators who know how to do this stuff, and put into the hands of people without the experience of knowing the importance of this responsibility.

Global Coordination

We're on a roll giving out DORG awards left and right. Good communication and coordination practices are essential in today's fast paced global environment. Communication is worse than ever in IT due mainly to this networked age of client/server computing and how things are distributed all over the world, becoming chaotic and uncontrollable. Once again the concept/idea of someone in charge of global coordination sounds good, but in reality you're introducing more bureaucracy and complexity into the organization.

We've seen the global coordinator or head of international support report to the CIO as well as the infrastructure group (see Figure 4–7). If you're bent on having such a position then we recommend having this person reporting into the infrastructure group just so their head doesn't swell. But it's also more important to coordinate infrastructure issues (i.e. connectivity, software distribution, hardware installations, production support, etc.) vs. Applications Development issues.

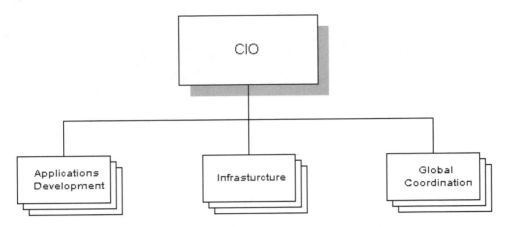

Figure 4–7 Ineffective global coordination.

We recommend that you not have a separate function to handle global coordination. It should be the responsibility of the infrastructure group to deal with their regional management who should be reporting to him/her.

Positioning the Help Desk

It's so critical to structure the help desk properly. It's not only the first point of contact for your customers, but the staff should be the owners of problem management which is one of the top three disciplines in IT. The other two are change control and production acceptance. The help desk needs to be structured at the enterprise level, nothing less and nothing more. This is easier said than done. One of the more commonly placed locations is under the desktop group as depicted in Figure 4–8.

We recommend that the help desk be structured at the enterprise level as depicted in Figure 4–9. The help desk needs to have authority and be able to support all groups equally.

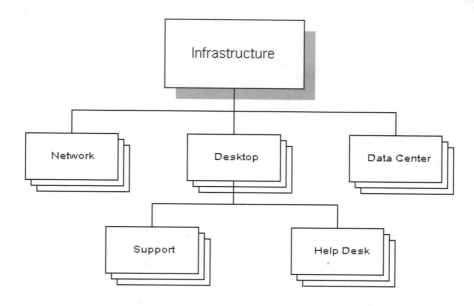

Figure 4–8 Common location of the help desk.

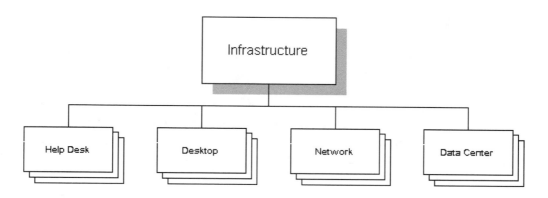

Figure 4–9 The help desk at the enterprise level

Desktop Support

We've seen so many variations of where and how desktop support should be structured. We have to give it a DORG award because people are working very hard trying to make things more confusing than they should be. The diagram in Figure 4–10 seems logical, especially to management, but for the troops in the trenches it's a nightmare. It's extremely difficult to separate hardware, software, and architecture. The help desk has a difficult time figuring out whom to call within the desktop support group because the functions overlap and confusion usually reigns.

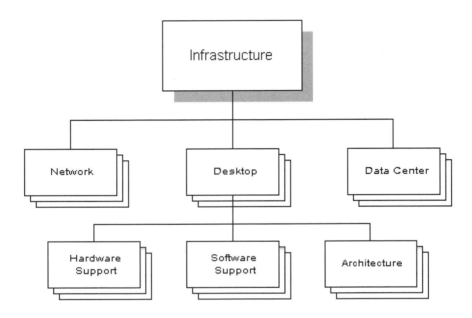

Figure 4–10 Undesirable desktop support structure.

Do not separate hardware and software support.

The Tape Librarian

The management of tape libraries will continue to be a critical function in the 21st century. Most IT production support groups today that support a client/server environment leave out the tape librarian function as a cost-reduction exercise. Put it back in! Never compromise data integrity! There must be one person dedicated to this function; it cannot be a part-time exercise performed by the operations staff.

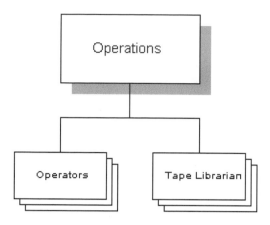

Figure 4–11 The tape librarian as part of the operations structure.

Most client/server operations supporting organizations today have done away with a person dedicated to ensuring data integrity. The Tape Librarian function was, and still is, essential (see Figure 4–11).

As we travel the globe doing our talks and assessments we often ask the question, can you guarantee that you can restore data from your backup tapes? The answer is always, "We think so." If you were to ask that same question to a mainframe organization—well, to tell you the truth, you would never ask them because it would be embarrassing to do so. Mainframe management would never have this type of worry.

Global Technologies

It's like having your own applications development staff for the infrastructure group (Figure 4–12). The only difference is that this group is a small—usually two or three people. Their main purpose in life is to focus on major initiatives (e.g., rolling out Microsoft Exchange around the world). The staff (permanent employees) should remain small. If for any reason the project is much larger in scope than this group can handle, consultants should be hired. In some shops we recommend this, and in others we do not. That's because sometimes the group has a tendency to grow too large. The individuals for this group are very senior technical staff, with a background in systems administration, applications development (Java, C+, etc.), and project planning.

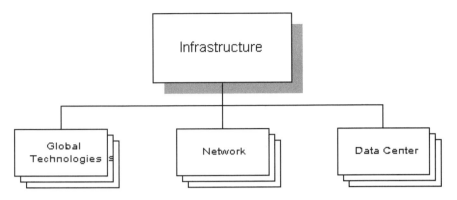

Figure 4–12   The global technologies group with the infrastructure.

Business Requirements First

Once again the intent is good, but we need to give it a huge DORG award. Not to be mean because it's an understandable mistake, but because it's a very costly mistake for the company. This scenario usually occurs when the head of IT comes from the business unit to head up IT. The typical structure is shown in Figure 4–13.

As an example, this structure would be supporting three distinct business units: Manufacturing, HR, and Finance. Each business unit would have a set of applications developers, usually one database administrator, and one system administrator. These are pretty much designed to be autonomous IT organizations. The intent is for the entire organization to work together, but in reality the priority and alliance is to the heads of Manufacturing, HR, or Finance. The operations box is the traditional centralized IT infrastructure support group.

The problems this structure causes are enormous:

- Systems management tools are not fully implemented; there is a lack of resources to properly implement tools.
- Senior system administrators spend 90 percent of their time on fire-fighting and daily problem resolution. They're left with only 10 percent of their time to plan, architect, and design the infrastructure that includes implementing system management solutions *but* for their own environment, *not* an enterprise solution. The goal should be 80 percent to plan, architect, and design enterprise solutions for the entire infrastructure, and 20 percent for problem resolution.

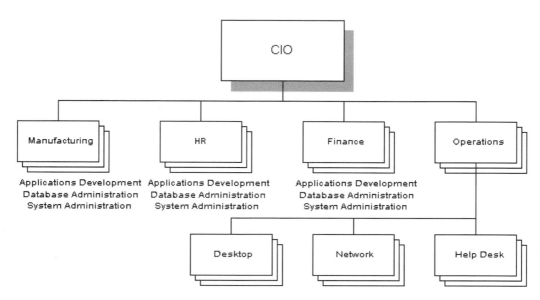

Figure 4–13 "Business requirements first" structure.

- Three levels of support not specified for system administration. They have resources for only one level of support.

- Lack of a centralized lape librarian function; each group handles its own tapes. There are very few (if any) procedures to assure integrity. This is extremely risky!

- Lack of a centralized computer operations function; senior system administrators are spending their time mounting tapes, monitoring systems/peripherals, etc. It is ludicrous for senior technicians to be wasting their time on such mundane tasks when they should be providing analysis on the latest and greatest technologies.

- Lack of a formalized applications support team (that role is partly filled by developers, DBAs, other individuals). Very little is formalized in the way of production support.

- Lack of a production control function. Once again, due to a lack of resources, this function does not exist, which means production QA, process ownership, second-level support structure is nonexistent.

- The help desk is not structured properly within the organization. It should be structured at the enterprise level and given the authority to own problem management.
- The organization is structured within silos focusing on particular technologies.
- Career development for Unix and database technical support staff is almost impossible in the current structure.
- Lack of processes.
- There is a general lack of discipline throughout the infrastructure.
- Finger pointing between the centralized IT operations staff and the autonomous groups.
- Teamwork and communication is less than adequate.

Our perception at first was that customer satisfaction was extremely high—more so than in the traditional IT organization structure. But that was not the case. In all the companies we visited, customer satisfaction was the same whether it was the traditional IT organization structure or this one.

The real proof is in the numbers, the industry average for System Administrators to mission-critical production servers is about 9 to 1 for good environments. The better environments are about 12 to 1. These autonomous IT organizations are averaging about 3 to 1—in some cases we saw 2 to 1. What would the CEO think? How much money is being wasted?

The Problems Short-Listed

How did these mainframe shops attain and maintain 99.9+ percent availability? Think about this question for a moment. How did the mainframe shops work so effectively compared to today's environments in which the client/server centers have every redundant component built into their systems? Anyone who purchases new Unix or NT servers is usually ordering these new machines with back-up power supplies, double power strips, extra RAID disks, etc. Just based on the product specifications alone, the newer systems should never, ever go down because they are double or triple packed. And most of the shops we visit gobble up this technology (with a healthy price tag) at an alarming rate. So why is client/server RAS non-existent? What's going on? The hardware is there. This isn't rocket science. The mainframe survived and is still excelling because of disciplines (organization structure, processes, metrics, etc.) which are enforced by the people who maintain the mainframes. The uptime isn't a result of the mainframe boxes themselves. The availability is caused by the mainframe support staff knowing what they are doing and doing it well. They have disciplines that should be used throughout the enterprise.

With all this technology available for redundancy comes complexity. The good news is that today we have more choices of components to use; call it "open systems." This means that we chose our databases, our utilities, our network vendors, and our operating systems. The bad news is that often these vendors' products don't easily plug and play together. Vendors *say* their products work well together. But when you need to make sure the versions are in synch, well, that's another matter. It's mainly a problem of making sure that the releases work well together which is one more reason to adopt key processes and deal with the people issues. If you rely on the technology only, which is what most IT shops do today, you will surely fail.

We recently visited a shop where the most critical system in the shop was down for over 24 hours and it started with a simple hardware problem. (Bad memory was the fault.) The hardware and software configuration had full fail-over capability. They were able to switch systems. They fixed the problem but as they switched back it corrupted a bunch of tables. It just went down hill from there. They needed to restore the database with the most recent backup. That tape was corrupted. They had to go back several weeks to find a good backup. There were no backup processes and procedures to test for integrity. There were no disaster-recovery procedures or periodic tests to restore data. To make a very long story short, there wasn't a tape librarian function. Instead of being down for a few hours, they were down for 24 hours. When the vendor sold the customer this multimillion-dollar solution, they guaranteed continuous operation.

Why is everyone in IT turning his or her back on an environment that supported mission critical like no other? We're referring to the mainframe world. Why does everyone want to reinvent the wheel or, as in most of the companies we studied, not invent the wheel at all? In this section we take a closer look at the most critical non-organizational-related issues with recommendations.

The Top Three Missing or Broken Processes

Now don't fall out of your chair when you read this. The top three missing or broken processes are:

1. Client/server production acceptance (CSPA)
2. Change control
3. Problem management

We can understand the first one because it only evolved over the past five years. But numbers two and three? They've been around for over two decades. This is pretty hard to swallow in this day and age.

Change control and problem management are two of the most critical processes or disciplines in data processing as depicted in Table 5–1. They're on top for a reason, namely that they are necessary to keep the organization flowing. For this reason we highlight them here, and go into further detail in the following pages.

The big problem is that three fourths of the companies we studied didn't even have an enterprise-wide change control process. Problem management was not as bad; 90 percent of the companies had something that resembled problem management. That's the good news, but the bad news is that 65 percent of them were broken. How can this be? Is anything and everything that ever came out of the mainframe environment tossed aside? Unfortunately, the answer appears to be yes. Seventy-five percent of the companies we studied had a legacy environment. Why is everyone turning his or her back to a very successful mission-critical, production-support environment? We can turn our back to many other aspects of the mainframe era but not the way it provides RAS. Once again that perception rears its ugly ageless head.

But there's so much more that's missing than just these three processes. The remaining issues are discussed later in this section.

Table 5–1 defines the components and processes for managing a disciplined production environment. The purpose of this diagram is to highlight the importance of the top three processes that are missing or broken in most computing environments.

Table 5–1 Components and Processes for Managing a Disciplined Production Environment

Client/Server Production Acceptance (CSPA)	Problem Management	Change Control	Service Level Agreements	
System and Network Security	Version Release Management	Network Management	Event Monitoring	Disaster Recovery
Capacity Planning	Performance Monitoring	Asset Management	Software Distribution	Job Scheduling
User Security Access	Console Management	Disk Management		

Lack of an Enterprise-wide Change Control Process

Change Control Process: *A process that coordinates any change that can potentially impact the operational production environment.*

Seventy-five percent of the companies we studied did not have an enterprise-wide, change control process. The ones that did had many problems. In Table 5–2 we highlight these problems and the percentage of occurrences from our elite group of 40.

Table 5–2   Problems with the Current Change Control Processes

Issues	Percent of Occurrences
Not all changes are logged.	95%
Changes not thoroughly tested.	90%
Lack of enforcement.	85%
Lack of effective method for communicating within IT.	75%
Coordination within the groups is poor—only the person attending the change meetings is aware of the events—on many occasions the information is not disseminated throughout the organization.	65%
Lack of centralized ownership.	60%
Change control is not effective. In some instances changes are being made on the production servers without coordination or communication.	60%
Lack of approval policy.	50%
Hard copies of 'changes' kept in file cabinets.	50%
On many occasions notification to all after the fact.	40%
Managers and directors sign a hard copy of every change.	25%
Current process is only a form for notification.	20%
The process is bureaucratic and not user-friendly.	20%
Several different flavors of change control.	20%

A change is any addition or modification to the data-processing systems that could potentially affect the stability of the production environment. Areas of change include, but are not limited to, hardware, system software (OS), application software, networks, environment (heating, cooling, and so on), and documentation.

When implementing change control, what is often overlooked, the fatal flaw in distributed systems, is not that you don't have enough controls and practices, but that there are not adequate checks and balances to detect unauthorized changes or unforeseen consequences. Checks and balances, especially for change control, help eliminate human error, improve the efficiency and effectiveness of the process, and ensure that we maintain high systems availability.

The basic elements in the change process are:

- Notification
- Review
- Approvals
- Scheduling
- Implementation

When a change to a production system (server, application, network, etc.) is required, the individual responsible for implementing the change fills out a form that documents the answers to the following questions:

- What's the business reason for change so it can be prioritized?
- When can it be done?
- When must it be done?
- What are the changes?
- What do they affect?
- Are there prerequisites and/or corequisites?
- Will the customer see the changes?
- How to communicate to customers?
- Will they change any of the operational parameters?
- How long will the change take?
- What is the status of the application-related applications, operating system, hardware, network, etc., during implementation of the change?
- What are the symptoms of the change not working properly?
- What will be the back-out procedure for the change?

- How long will the back-out take?
- What is the status of the application-related applications, operating system, hardware, network, etc., during the back-out?

Once the form has been completed the individual acquires the proper approvals, and then has to submit it to a group that owns the change control process. Changes are then reviewed and approved weekly. Bureaucratic? Sure it is. That's because properly-designed checks and balances, when used, mitigate risk. We want to minimize problems, avoid Murphy's Law of everything going wrong, to maintain RAS.

Secure? Hardly, because regardless of any process that looks good on paper, certain individuals have the capability of making changes to the environment without following the process. A good example of this is a mainframe systems programmer. This individual could make a change to the MVS operating system whenever he/she wanted. They owned the key to the box. So why bother going through all this? What's the point? Because the MIS staff was mentored in disciplines and this type of behavior was unheard of.

To ease the bureaucratic delays and paper shuffling that can bog down controlled changes, the entire approval process, including authorizing signatures, can be put on e-mail. The person requesting a system change fills out a change request (online) script. The change request describes the proposed change and the impact it will have on the system, which unit or group owns the server, any special change instructions, and what procedures to take to back out of the change if it fails.

Another option to ease paper shuffling, as well as managerial nerves, might be an automated, online Web-based bulletin board that lets users see which requests are pending for approval, which have been approved but are awaiting implementation, and systems changes up to a month old. Additionally, this application can have alerts that can e-mail change-control documents and updates regularly to IT personnel. Your goal should be to track and communicate (via e-mail) each and every change affecting your production environment. This process provides discipline, an audit trail for accountability, and mitigates risk so that IT's customers have a greater level of satisfaction.

Next, you can automatically monitor those servers to detect changes by using a simple command in Unix to compare a before and after snapshot of a server. The results are stored in a database for review by staff and management. You should know exactly what changes have been made to any server in the past 24 hours and who made them.

By storing all information in a database, retrieving information or audit trails by server will be simplified and accurate.

Lack of an Effective Problem Management Process

Problem Management Process: *A centralized process to manage and resolve user, network, application, and system problems.*

Ninety percent of the companies we studied have some sort of problem management process, but many of them were riddled with problems as depicted in Table 5–3.

Table 5–3   Problem Management Issues

Issues	Percentage of Occurrences
Customer satisfaction isn't measured after problem is resolved. (None of the companies we surveyed had a post-resolution customer survey process!)	100%
Multiple levels of support are not clearly defined for client/server environments.	100%
Support personnel have very little exposure to new systems when deployed.	95%
Level 2 analysts not putting in detailed description of problem resolution.	90%
Lack of written documentation on existing and new systems/applications.	90%
Roles and responsibilities not clearly defined for problem resolution.	90%
Service levels of the companies studied not defined for problem resolution.	90%
Lack of root-cause analysis.	85%
Help desk staff not properly trained on new releases of applications.	80%
Lack of centralized ownership.	70%
Lack of close-loop feedback.	70%
Lack of metrics (performance or quality incentives).	65%
Problems not followed through to closure.	60%

Table 5–3   Problem Management Issues

Issues	Percentage of Occurrences
Perception is that the help desk is not responsive.	50%
Problem tracking is poor, leaving the user without a clear understanding of who owns the problem and how to follow up on the resolution process.	50%
Most of the Unix or NT problems bypass the help desk—going directly to senior technical staff instead.	50%
Not one common enterprise-wide problem management process i.e., escalation—each group has its own requirements (e.g.,"Don't call me between the hours of X and X on Saturday night, call X.").	40%
HelpdDesk staff has very little authority.	40%
Many calls bypass the help desk.	35%
Lack of clear demarcation for problem resolution between desktop and LAN group.	30%
Help desk acts more like a dispatch center, leaving users frustrated, feeling like they simply get the runaround while no one is willing to solve problems.	30%
Not clearly defined for after-hours support in the client/server environment.	25%
Escalation not clearly understood.	20%
Problems not documented by help desk personnel.	20%
The process is extremely bureaucratic. A high number of notification and escalation procedures.	15%
Sometimes problems just sit around for days or weeks.	15%
On-call list is on the mainframe, but not everyone has mainframe access.	10%

The purpose of problem management is to establish an ongoing process to resolve problems, minimize the impact affecting IT services, and optimize the time and effort spent in resolution. The roblem management process facilitates immediate resolution without wasting time to figure out how to manage a problem. This is achieved by setting into motion a management process that encompasses an "interdepartmental" problem effort that will effectively manage the measurements of a tracking, escalation, resolution and reporting system (see the process flow diagram in Figure 5–1.)

The lack of a full problem management solution hinders IT from its ability to measure service delivery and manage its customer base; thus customer service is actually limited. It also makes it difficult for IT to manage scarce resources because it is difficult to gauge where time is being spent firefighting rather than providing active service. Because users are calling technical staff directly, very little time is left to keep abreast and plan for new technologies.

As a side note, we were shocked to find that some of the companies we surveyed didn't have established problem management processes in place in their IT shops. Some of these companies, however, have been highlighted in numerous news stories and books on how their public relations staffs handle major problems such as disasters, customer complaints, or customer returns. Ironic, isn't it?

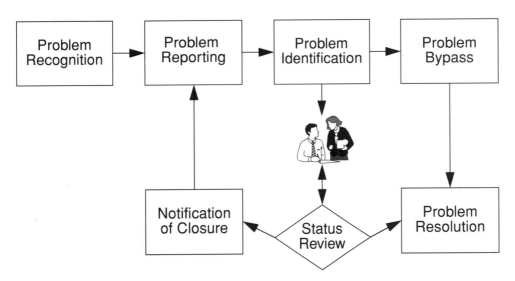

Figure 5–1   Problem management process.

Lack of a Production Acceptance Process

Production Acceptance Process: *A methodology to promote communication, standards, guidelines, and teamwork for deploying, implementing, and supporting mission critical client/server distributed systems.*

The Client/server production acceptance (CSPA) process is also an operations runbook, service level agreement, and a working document defining everyone's roles and responsibilities for each new client/server production application. It is the QA process for production. The process should also be used for all major revisions to applications.

The CSPA will provide development and operations with the adhesive needed to bring the development and support parties together through structured communication and by setting expectations to implement and support mission-critical applications. The CSPA provides a checklist of requirements needed for operational groups to support a system installation in production. The CSPA also specifies everyone's roles and responsibilities for supporting mission-critical systems.

The CSPA is the cornerstone of all processes. We've been preaching about the needs for and benefits of this process since our first book, *Rightsizing the New Enterprise*, which we published in 1994. In the book we referred to this process as the Unix Production Acceptance (UPA) process. Very few companies use such a tool. In one of our earlier books in the Enterprise Institute Series, *Software Development (Building Reliable Systems)* (Prentice-Hall), we introduced the Web-centric Production Acceptance Process. We estimate only 10 percent (and that's being generous) in the industry use a production acceptance process to manage their enterprise. Sad, but it's true. Out of the 40 Fortune 1000 companies we studied for this book, only a few had something like it.

Everywhere we go executives talk about improving communications, but this is easier said than done. Doing it effectively is a whole different ballgame. Improving communications has to be driven by a process. Monthly meetings and quarterly get-togethers don't cut it. You need to have a single process to monitor service levels which covers topics such as:

- User requirements
- Business issues
- New applications
- Revisions to existing applications
- Services provided, etc.

But don't burden these poor users with several different bureaucratic processes. They're trying to do more with less as well. What's needed is a single process to promote and instill effective communication practices. We discuss this process, which we refer to as production acceptance, in several books: *Rightsizing the New Enterprise, Managing the New Enterprise*, and *Building the New Enterprise*.

Although the name is misleading, it is so much more than a production acceptance process. Its primary focus is to instill and promote effective communication practices internally within IT and a process for IT to effectively communicate with its users on a daily basis. This is done by adhering to the CSPA checklist for each application being deployed into a production environment. It is a constant reminder to bring the groups together within IT and the customers to assure proper system deployment.

The Other Issues

Lack of Metrics

Not one of the companies we studied had organization-wide metrics. About half of the companies had some sort of help desk metrics, and the 75 percent that had mainframe systems had some form of metrics for them.

There is a lack of metrics to measure effectiveness in the client/server environment. That old saying holds true here, if you can't measure it, there's no way you can manage it effectively. It is also important to establish internal metrics for each area of the operation, as well as quarterly or semi-annual ratings to compare the results based on cost and performance efficiencies. When these companies get their infrastructure in order it's imperative that they establish metrics. For more information on establishing metrics see our book entitled *Building the New Enterprise*.

The general use of metrics is imperative to the overall running of the IT department. Using a service such as Gartner Group to evaluate your organization is a constructive use of budget dollars. This is not to say that it is an annual expense, yet it is good for the IT department to compare its cost and performance efficiencies to other similar operations in and out of their industry.

Benchmarking Information Technology Services

The next step is to document the extent of services and their related costs so that you can compare them. The idea is to compare the cost of System Administration support or Network support with vendors providing this type of service. Tear your infrastructure apart in pieces. Then go out and benchmark. Ask them what they would charge to support your mission-critical servers, network, and so on. This is only a benchmark exercise, as outsourcing any part of your client/server mission-critical environment is not recommended. Once your infrastructure is cost-effective, take a look at your competition. For additional information on benchmarking your environment read our book titled *Building the New Enterprise*.

Poor Communications

With the evolution of client/server computing and the torrid pace of change with Information Technology, maybe this section should read "No communications." In the spirit of doing more with less—who has the time? And if by some small miracle you find the time, to whom do you turn? In this networked era there are no clear demarcations as to who does what to whom and when. And this is only internally within IT. What about the poor users? Are we effectively communicating with them? You can answer that one. Very few IT shops are even measuring customer satisfaction. Only a couple of the 40 companies we analyzed actually attempted to measure customer satisfaction. This is atrocious! But we understand the frustrations with the old process of sending out survey forms every quarter. Scheduled survey forms aren't popular and the usual response rate is less than 30 percent. There are ways to reengineer this entire process (see our book *Rightsizing the New Enterprise*). It is a must!

Not Fully Implemented Systems Management Tools

Systems management is critical to successful daily operations of the client/server environment. It is also an important resource for the planning of future activities. Systems management tools gather data that can be saved and used to determine trends. So, they are not only valuable to daily monitoring of system activities, but they provide other benefits.

On a daily basis, systems management can save the organization. Monitoring tools are as important today as they were with standalone mainframes. The difference is that with so many computer complexes running programs and passing data from platform to platform, systems management tools help isolate the problem. Remember that client/server means distributed programs and data. What better way to isolate a problem than with systems management tools?

In every company we studied, systems management tools are not being fully implemented. The gap between their potential use and their actual use ranged from 90 percent to 30 percent, meaning that the tools weren't being fully used. The systems management tools in the majority of these companies (80 percent) are not implemented by as much as 50 percent. This is a real sad statistic. One of the primary reasons the mainframe environment is so successful in maintaining RAS is because systems management tools are fully implemented, customized, and maintained.

Systems management tool vendors haven't changed much. They promise the world with each and every product, regardless of the platform. We all know it's hogwash that the vendors claim their products require very little effort for installation or maintenance. The reality is that these tools take a heck of a lot of effort to implement, customize and maintain. As we discuss throughout this book, it's the organization structure that causes this problem. The current structures do not allow the proper time for senior technicians to effectively do what they're good at doing, which is providing enterprise-wide, system management solutions. To be successful, you're going to have to devote time and resources to make these tools work.

Lack of Senior Technical Resources

The number of technologies in the computing environment today is unprecedented. You need senior technical staff to implement and maintain these technologies, and to know how they interact.

All of the 40 IT organizations we surveyed complained about not having adequate technical resources. For a quarter of these companies it was a legitimate beef. They were scarce on senior technical resources and finding talented help has become increasingly more difficult. Most of their efforts are being spent on external recruiting. This should continue, but there must be breeding within the organization as well. The current organization structures do not promote effective technical career development. This needs to be a priority.

In many instances, what happens after someone works his or her way up through the ranks, having been trained by the organization, is that he or she seeks free agency out in the marketplace where the rewards are very lucrative for technical personnel. This can never be completely prevented. Our answer is that it's better to have this individual on board for a few years than not to have them at all.

Retaining staff needs to be a focus as well. But as you can see with all the problems highlighted in Table 2–1, especially the daily firefighting routine with no end in sight, this is a monumental task. The sooner that you resolve the organizational issues with three levels of support and an effective problem management process, the better off your IT group will be. This would allow some time for your senior technical staff to perform some architecture and design functions, not to forget about playing with the latest and greatest technology in the marketplace.

Transitioning and Mentoring Legacy Staff

Due to the scarcity of technical resources, transitioning and mentoring existing legacy staff is paramount. You've got to have a developmental plan, if for no other reason than to entice your personnel to stay and not go down the block. This is often a difficult management decision. Does an IT manager spend money on training employees and run the risk of losing them to a competitor for a better employment package, or do we spend the money with the confidence that they will not take the training and run?

Employees will come and go, and if the working environment is challenging and the management is fair, the chances are very good that the employee is going to stay. We found that many IT organizations don't distribute the training and education evenly throughout the employment ranks. Some employees received the lion share of the training and others were neglected.

One of the most important ingredients and biggest challenges in transitioning to client/server distributed computing is motivating the mainframe professionals to adopt and adapt to this new networked environment. They need special guidance and special projects on which to work. They need to be involved in the planning and implementation of your heterogeneous infrastructure while maintaining RAS in the legacy environment.

There are several reasons why this is so important. Mainframe staff are trained and disciplined in supporting a controlled and managed environment. To successfully transition to a client/server environment, you want to include mainframe staff in your new paradigm. It's easier to teach mainframe staff a new technology than it is to teach discipline to client/server technical staff. Their disciplined mentoring is critical to building a world-class client/server environment.

Another key factor in favor of retraining and transitioning mainframe staff versus hiring replacement talent is that they know the business. Last, and probably the most critical, is to sustain morale. It takes everyone working together to make this transition successful. Providing the organization with at least the opportunity to learn is important. The ones with the initiative and drive will take advantage of these programs. The ones that won't will have nothing to complain about as long as they were provided the opportunity. It is imperative that you establish a curriculum to break the mindset barriers between the legacy and newer distributed environments. You may want to consider the following programs:

- **Vendor-sponsored events on technology trends in the marketplace.** Technology is evolving at a torrid pace. Use your hardware or software vendor to share those trends with your organization on a monthly basis.

  Like everyone else in the industry, you're probably inundated with dozens of invitations to vendor seminars every month. Neither you nor your staff has the time to attend these events. So, ask the vendors to visit you. We recommend that you use hardware and software vendors to provide monthly lunchtime seminars on the latest and greatest in technology. Make these sessions mandatory for your staff. Keep them relatively short, under 90 minutes, and tell the vendors that you want them to minimize the marketing hyperbole and concentrate on the applicability of their solutions to your environment. In other words, you want them to have to think about how their products can help you solve your problems, not just make their sales figures look good. You might ask the vendor if his or her company uses the products to run their business. If they do, suggest that they send a representative of their IT department to meet with you to talk about how to use the tools or products in a day-to-day operating environment. The vendor will jump at the opportunity to showcase its latest and greatest products. Management should also track in monthly status reports who attends each session.

- **Get acquainted with the hardware and OS.** The mainframe has always received preferential mission-critical treatment, and for good reason. In the seventies and early eighties that type of thinking was warranted. Nowadays that association needs to carry forward throughout the enterprise. We recommend a program consisting of a half-day classroom session to understand the hardware (servers). The second half of the class should be hands-on in the data center (their own habitat) in which teams of three to five students (staff from different functional groups) take apart new servers and then put them back together again. This does wonders for the mindset and promotes the fact that a production system is a production system regardless of the box, not to mention promoting teamwork.

- **Professional technical training.** Pick a minimum set of classes for a particular organization. For your production support personnel, pick a minimum of three courses. Make sure you include classes on systems administration and script programming. Provide this minimal set to all data center employees. If you exclude people, you will start having morale problems and that's something you don't want to experience. The point is to increase morale.

  Script programming is included in the equation because you just don't send people to training without having them involved in real projects. Writing and editing of scripts are essential skills for Unix systems management. So that your senior technical staff members can learn to apply their years of experience maintaining and performance-tuning mainframes to Unix-based systems, you should also require several other essential courses for them, including C++ Programming, Advanced Systems Administration, Operating Systems Internals, etc.

- **Hands-on projects.** Look at all the manual processes you have in place today. Put your Unix system administrators and mainframe personnel on projects together to create scripts to automate manual processes and eliminate as much of the bureaucracy as possible. This should be done on their personal time and will provide management with insight as to who has the initiative and drive to move forward.

A good example of a manual process that's still being used today in a mainframe data center, or any fairly large 24×7 environment, is called "shift turnover." This manual process usually is nothing more than a piece of paper on a clipboard explaining special requests for a night's production processing. This process covers anything out of the ordinary the operations staff must know. Once all the special requests are completed and signed off, this paper is put into a file cabinet. This is a good process, but manual and bureaucratic. Why not have your operations staff work on a project to automate this process? Call it `shift` so that from your desktop a script appears with the night's special processing requirements. When completed, the requirements get e-mailed to the appropriate parties and, once completed, the sequence of work is filed in an online database.

- **Train the trainer.** Your lead systems administrator should be the first person to go through the training programs. Once he or she completes the program, the rest of your mainframe staff will follow suit. They have to be convinced that you are committed to the programs. To make sure the programs are the right ones for retraining your mainframers, who better but your best and most respected systems programmer to help you along the right track and lead the others down the path of client/server computing? It is essential that this person display initiative and drive.

- **Brown bag lunchtime seminars.** This newly-trained individual can also hold weekly lunchtime sessions on different topics. Each topic should have homework assignments that are to be done on staff member's own time. Establish a special lab with servers, where students can complete assignments that can vary from reconfiguring hardware to modifying the operating system. It's important to have one of your own employees do this because it brings the group together. Do not hire a consultant to do this!

- **Invest in a lab for your staff.** You don't want your IT operations staff toying with production servers or even those that are designated for applications development. You want to give your operations staff its own lab with its own servers to test the hardware and OS. The servers don't have to be the latest and greatest. In fact, talk with your vendors about purchasing or leasing refurbished gear. You'll save money and yet have ample hardware to support the versions of the OS you have in production.

- **Books.** Provide staff with a list of books to read on their own time. Pick the top two or three books on networking, database administration, system administration, and so on. Maintain a current book list. One script writing project could be to make the reading list accessible on the Web.

- **Metrics.** Track the students' performance. Include the students' progress through the training courses each month in your status report to senior management. If you've implemented a dashboard of metrics for your organization, include training as one of the gauges. So, if an employee has a performance problem—as determined through other Human Resources-sanctioned evaluations—you could easily see if the cause was insufficient training. It is more of a CYA than anything else. This employee could run to HR and complain of insufficient training programs while the organization is transitioning to support a more heterogeneous mission-critical production environment. As long as you track all assignments, programs completed, homework, books read, etc., there won't be anything to discuss with HR.

- **Job descriptions.** Establish one generic job description for each function, which includes all technologies. (See Appendix A in our book titled *Building the New Enterprise*.)

Internal Support Agreement

The differences between applications development and operational support are well documented. Even when evelopment and operations were centralized, fingerpointing was common. There weren't many options and most IT professionals opted to pass the buck rather than face the music. Networked client/server computing has changed all that.

Most of the issues were always around implementation and support of mission-critical applications. Development would blame operations for messing up a restart to an *abend* or operations would blame development for lack of QA or support on their part. There were many issues of this nature.

In most companies today, applications development is located within the business unit or division for business reasons. This is good for quickly responding to business issues and requirements, but creates additional friction between the groups.

At Sun Microsystems, where two of the three authors worked during the transformation from mainframe to client/server computing, we not only went through decentralization, but we dealt with cultural differences. Many of our new development staff came from a Unix or client/server background. And we had a number of people on board who had been in the legacy world.

The development organization still wanted centralized IT to support their servers for system administration types of functions such as backups and restores, so it's not much different than the old way of doing business when operations would support the development environment on the mainframe.

At first, our development staff attempted to support their own servers. Well, they tried. They wanted to do things their way. They enjoyed the freedom of being on their own and having root authority (security privileges). Reality set in when it was time to perform system administration functions on a consistent basis (backups, O/S maintenance, etc.). But who wants to? That sort of stuff is boring. Operations support has been providing these services for years.

The first meeting we had with one of our development groups was memorable. We met with a manager and two of his senior technical staff. One topic that we discussed was who would own root functionality to their Development environment.

It started out as a pleasant discussion. We had worked with this manager in the past and there was a mutual respect. He requested that we perform system administration functions while his organization keep root. We stated (in true dictatorial fashion) that the only way to effectively perform system administration functions and to maintain integrity is for the data center to own root. They said, oh no, we must own root. It would tie our hands and slow us down from effectively performing our job. We knew this conversation wasn't going anywhere. Why argue? So we played along with their request, giving them root authority and we'd perform the support role. We knew that within days they would clobber their environment, and they did just that. We came back and told them that the only way they could maintain high reliability, availability, and serviceability with the limited resources we had was to own root. They said that it was essential for performing their job. We were sympathetic and understood the deadlines and pressure they were under. We came back and said that we no longer wanted to perform these system administration functions because of this issue. The conversation was going nowhere. But then, for whatever reason (maybe frustration), we eased up and said, OK, let's try something as an experiment—joint root authority. The data center will own it and two of your senior technical staff will own it as well. If the developers abused this policy, the data center would no longer support their servers. Everyone agreed! Eight years later and it's still working. A sample ISA (the original one which was developed in 1990) is included in Appendix C.

External Service Agreement

The entire concept of service agreements evolved once again from those mainframe environments. In its inception, the sole purpose of what MIS referred to as a service level agreement (SLA) was a contract between the IT department and its end-users. All service related expectations were outlined in black and white. The following was recorded and monitored:

- Online availability
- Response times
- Report deliveries
- Problem resolution expectations
- Special requests for services, etc.

Many shops still use this SLA, and we've included one in Appendix B. The only problem with this process is that once the document is signed and heralded by all participants, in many instances it just gets put on a shelf somewhere to gather dust. What we recommend is to incorporate the function of the SLA into the CSPA process for each application. The CSPA is an active process that promotes and instills effective communication practices.

Learn from the Past to Build the Future

We're no different than anyone else in IT. We didn't want to believe that anything that evolved out of the mainframe world would actually be beneficial in this networked era (e.g., processes, methodologies, etc.). And why would anyone ever think that the mainframe organization structure would work for any other paradigm? Not a chance! Many of us have this negative perception and remember all the bureaucracy that came out of that environment. But the process bureaucracy had nothing to do with how effective the organization structure was. The structure empowered the people.

We'll be the first to admit that we were embarrassed to tell the truth with the results of our assessment findings because we were labeled the client/server infrastructure doctors. What would the world think of us if we praised the mainframe organization structure? We knew the answer. There was a pattern after the fifth assessment but we chose not to write about it until after 40 assessments.

Why was that organizational structure so successful? The way they split the organization in half was ingenious. There was mission critical and everything else. All energy was focused on mission-critical 24×7 support. They came up with a masterpiece and called it the Data Center. A true work of art! The perception is that it was established and had evolved around the mainframe. The mainframe organization structure was established to provide 24×7 mission-critical support. The focus was not on hardware or technology. It was mission-critical! One might argue there wasn't as much technology around then. We remember that in our data center there was an Amdahl and a Hitachi mainframe, HP 3000 minicomputers, and other systems. People from all over the world continuously knock the mainframe environment for it's bureaucracy, inflexibility, and costly ways. But rarely does anyone speak of the good that came out of this environment. The good is what we learned about maintaining RAS. We also learned about:

- Disciplines
- Production support structure
- Production control function
- Process ownership and support for processes like change control and problem management.
- Standards
- Security
- High availability
- Selecting and fully implementing system management tools
- Service level agreements
- Architecture/planning
- Metrics

There are many key areas to which we should pay homage, but none as important as the organization structure itself. Some might beg to differ, but the preceeding issues could only be handled with the proper organization structure. It took years for the mainframe executives to get it right, and what they got right was an organization structure to best support RAS. As we review the elements that make up that organization, ask yourself if your IT organization has brought forward these components to support today's networked environment.

The Organization

Production Control

The first function to which we need to pay homage in the legacy environment was referred to as production control, which provided us with:

- *Second-level production support*. These were—and still are—the primary areas where problems were introduced to MIS after the problems were detected or raised to the first level. The first level was the help desk and/or computer operations. Second-level production support were junior technical staff (i.e., operations analysts in the mainframe world), one level above computer operators. Eighty percent of problem determination was handled by these people first.

  The goal was to resolve at least 80 percent of the problems before they reached those computing gods of the seventies and eighties, the very elite mainframe systems programmer (third-level support). We were developing their skill set to become system programmers (third-level support).

  Heaven forbid that problems be turned over to them before every possible attempt was made to resolve the problem. They had chips on their shoulders and an attitude bigger than their mainframe. No one wanted to disturb them from designing, building, and maintaining their infrastructure.

- *Assistance to senior technical staff in the analysis, implementation, and customization of enterprise-wide system management tools*. It takes at least one for each type of discipline (tape backup, security, etc.). We would pair a very senior person and one junior person to work together. Once trained, junior administrators can take ownership and provide maintenance on the tool. We can learn a couple of lessons from this arrangement. One, the pairing of senior and junior staff provides a mentoring process so that less experienced staff can learn on the job, which builds overall competency and individual skill sets. Second, systems-management tools aren't that easy to implement and maintain, as we alluded to earlier in the book, despite what the vendors may claim. Remember, our survey showed that most companies fail to use the full potential of the tools, so take advantage of their capabilities. It helps to devote resources to their use.

- *Assistance to senior technical staff in providing junior system administration functions* (i.e., O/S support, hardware setup, on-call support, etc.). Senior technical staff should not get bogged down with day-to-day maintenance functions.

- *Production quality assurance function.* No system was put into production before its time.

- *Process ownership* (e.g., change control, problem management, etc.) There can be only one owner.

Systems Programming

The second area we need to eternally bless is the system programmer function. RAS evolved mostly from this function. Without this elite organization there would be no RAS. These pros provided the high-level planning/architecture function. For decades there wasn't a separate architecture function. The Systems Programmers were also the ones to resolve unique problems which no one else in the organization could figure out.

In today's environment most Fortune 500 companies have a separate architecture function. In the 1970s and 1980s this function was imbedded within the technical services or technical support staff. These people were the visionaries and planners in building that Fort Knox of computing we refer to as the data center. The big difference between the systems programmer of the past and today's architect is that one listens to the users and shmoozes with senior management while the other could not care less. Those ancient yet highly respected system programmers built things the way they saw fit. They didn't do the politically correct things, they just did the right things and did they do a great job of it. OK, they may have aggravated the users. It was not their forte to market and sell IT services, or do/say the politically correct things. But, boy, could they build an infrastructure! Going forward into the new century, the objective should be to combine the background skills of the systems administrators with the business acumen of today's applications development specialists. We want to get the best of both cultures, so to speak, so that new applications will be developed with a wholesome attitude and concern for RAS as well as solving business problems for IT's customers.

Given enough time, many people can build an infrastructure. There's no reason in the world why system administrators today couldn't do the same. But they aren't given the time or opportunity. Unfortunately, this isn't a priority. Priorities have changed. As we mentioned earlier, building the proper infrastructure is secondary to new development initiatives. And, to make matters worse, CIOs don't have a clear understanding of what's going on in the trenches of their own infrastructure. The people and process issues are out of control right in their own back yard and they don't even know it. But it's not their fault. They're too busy working and understanding the business issues, listening and politicking with the users, and shmoozing big time with corporate executives. The outside consultants, for the most part, aren't concerned with the infrastructure either. The big consulting firms' experts focus on applications and business issues, not infrastructure processes. How many big five consultants do you know who came out of MIS or IT organizations where they were responsible for RAS? Not many, we're willing to wager.

Database Administration

The DBA group is responsible for supporting the database functions of applications. They take ownership of database servers and software.

Database administration has typically carried two meanings. One is the design, definition, and support of the logical database. The second is the design, definition, and support of the physical database. In the age of monolithic mainframe computing solutions, a single person or staff filled these roles. This was facilitated by the database design being developed in a hierarchical method. Therefore, relationships between objects were defined in a parent-child type of structure. This allowed for a centralized computing environment with centralized staff. As the technology moves from glass-house computer room environments to distributed server-room installations, the purpose of database administration has also changed. Databases are now predominately in a relational database model. This requires design/definition issues to be an integral part of application development.

This is expected to continue with object oriented technology as well. As such, the logical database administration tasks fall within a development group and the physical database administration tasks belong to an operations/support organization. The following attempts to outline roles/responsibilities/considerations of physical database administration in distributed environments.

Database environments should be distributed to allow information, which is critical to the success of a given organization, to be located as close to the user group as physically possible. This allows the production environment to be more reliable due to the removal of multiple points of failure. For example, if the user community which is primarily responsible for the data is located in Boston, and the server is in Colorado, the users have to traverse a myriad of network connections in order to play their transactions. This means that if a network connection goes out in Chicago, the transaction will either be queued or re-routed through a less expedient path. In the event of a lack of redundancy for every network connection, the user will most probably get a message of failed transactions. Then the transactions will have to be replayed later. For environments that involve a high number of user transactions, a remote location could involve network saturation and a high rate of collisions. This would also affect the response time to the user and that could be detrimental to business success. These are a few of the reasons why production environments should be distributed. However, a distributed environment does not eliminate chaos.

Every distributed server needs to be configured with a minimum set of requirements as well. It is important that production environments adhere to some configuration standards in order to leverage the highest DBA-to-server ratios. In the event of database outages or errors, you want a DBA to quickly access the machines, navigate through the file system structure and obtain information necessary to quickly take corrective action.

If the directory structure for the production machines is not established according to guidelines, there will be a further delay in problem diagnosis and resolution.

The role of a database administrator includes responsibilities in the areas of performance and tuning. Most performance gains can be found in the process of application and logical database design. However, there are tuning procedures that can be done by the database administrator to optimize performance across the physical resources of the production server. For example, allocating data space and index space across separate devices and device controllers can prevent bottlenecks. In order to accomplish this tuning function, the DBA needs access to programs and routines that can collect performance statistics on an as-needed basis. There are programs available that can track logical and physical writes and reads on an object-by-object basis for the popular database environments such as Oracle, Sybase and DB2.

Remember back when the DBA function was centralized under one organization, providing IT related services throughout the entire corporation? Just like any other IT function (networking, operations, etc.), providing service was the primary responsibility. It really didn't matter to which group they provided those services. Their charter was and still is to design, implement, and maintain the corporate databases. It's an atrocity to see what's happened to this function over the past decade. The political atmosphere of being decentralized has caused more bickering than the Democrats and Republicans.

DBAs have been restructured into the business unit, in Applications Development, in Operations, and in some companies they are spread out everywhere. Tables 6–1, 6–2, and 6–3 list the positive and negative aspects of the DBA function being decentralized or centralized.:

Table 6–1   DBA Decentralized into the Business Unit

Positive	Negative
Priority and focus for the business unit.	Lack of common standards.
Faster turnaround for Database implementations.	Lack of enterprise-wide Database Administration solutions.
A better understanding of the business.	Usually very thin on resources.
	RAS compromised—definitely not a priority.
	Wasted corporate costs because each BU is doing their own thing—Integration, tools, etc. are a big issue.

Table 6–2   DBA Located Within Applications Development

Positive	Negative
Focus is on design and development of the database.	Performance and tuning issues are not a top priority.
	Following standards is not a priority.

Table 6–2 DBA Located Within Applications Development

Positive	Negative
	Poor communication with DBAs providing production support.

Table 6–3 DBA Located Within Operations or Production Support

Positive	Negative
Adherence to standards.	Business units will not get the same priority as if they had their own DBA.
Pooling of resources.	May not have the same understanding for that particular business.
Enhancement of career/skills development.	
Design, plan, and architect the proper databases.	
Cost effective.	
Performance and tuning issues addressed up-front.	

We reiterate that this function has to be one of the most politically sensitive in IT. We're well aware of the popular clamor in the industry calling for every development group to have its own DBA or two. From our analysis, seeing operations across the globe, we know that this thinking may be popular but the results are not good; in fact, this whole idea is ludicrous. Just because the perception is that a particular business unit or division is not receiving preferential treatment doesn't mean that IT executives should give up the goal of RAS. Give us a break! The DBA's function is to serve! And let's not forget, those DBAs of yesteryear provided some awesome high-RAS databases (IDMS, IMS, etc.) that served multiple divisions or departments in their organizations.

If centralizing DBAs is not the right answer for your company, or the political atmosphere will never allow this, then what we recommend is for the DBAs to reside in business units but report directly to a centralized DBA group within Operations. The other scenario (not our top choice) is to have the same DBA who reports to the business unit also report to a centralized DBA group on a dotted-line basis.

Three Levels of Support

Whoever came up with three levels of support within the organization was a genius. This is one of the best structures ever designed and probably the single most important reason the mainframe world was so successful. First the roles of this structure:

Level 1: Monitor the systems (servers, network, peripheral devices), first-level problem determination, and resolution attempt. After an N number of minutes, as determined by the problem management process, the problem will be escalated to second-level support.

Level 2: Problem determination and attempted resolution. After N minutes as determined by the problem management process, the problem will be escalated to third level. A side note: There was a fear of escalating to the third level. The group's goal was to do everything possible to resolve the problem here before escalating to the senior gurus of the department. Senior System Administrators are worth their weight in gold. The entire organization needs to protect this valuable resource.

Level 3: The buck stops here. If they couldn't fix the problem, then no one could.

The benefits from this structure were enormous:

- First and foremost, this structure allowed senior technical staff the opportunity to architect and design a reliable, available, and serviceable infrastructure. The goal should be for first and second-level support staff to handle 80 percent of the problems before escalation.
- Skills for junior and second-level support personnel are enhanced. Organizations today need to breed senior technical staff within the organization as quickly as possible, and continue with their external recruitment efforts.
- Better turnaround for problem resolution.

- The ability to fully provide analysis and implementation of enterprise systems management solutions.

Computer Operations

Computer operators did so much more 20 years ago than just monitor the computing environment. They:

- Assisted in every facet of infrastructure development and support.
  - System management implementations
  - Disaster recovery
  - Data center hardware installs
  - Print management
- Assisted second- and third-level support with facilities management.
- Provided a higher level of problem determination and resolution.
- Provided a solid tape librarian function. This function played a key role in disaster recovery testing.

What's happened to us? Why are we in IT abandoning all these resources? These were individuals who were mentored to be part of all RAS efforts. They were given responsibilities that would enhance their career development. We used everyone to his or her utmost capabilities!

Processes

Process Development and Implementation

Why aren't processes flourishing in client/server computing? When we speak with managers around the globe they all speak of technology, technology, and more technology. Why aren't they preaching processes, processes, and more processes? And more important, why aren't these processes imbedded deep into the bowels of the infrastructure? Even the basic processes (change control, problem management, etc.) are not thriving as depicted in Table 5–1.

Some executives are aware of this, so they organize a special group reporting into the management of the infrastructure group to focus on process development. This brings up another set of issues and problems. What we've seen in many companies is that this group is headed up by a very small staff. At times this group is led by a person who used to manage a larger group and, for whatever reason, it didn't work out. Yet this individual had some good qualities so "we'll put him here." Another scenario would be for an individual to head this group who came from somewhere other than the trenches within the infrastructure. This is a huge mistake and a common problem in the industry. The issues with having a separate group other than your own technical production support staff lead this endeavor are enormous:

- Buy-in is difficult when it's done outside of the group that needs to adhere to it.
- The staff removed from the trenches don't really understand the details. You had to have been reared in that type of environment.

Back in the mainframe days, processes were developed and implemented by system programmers, database administrators, operations analysts, etc. These same people maintained and made sure that everyone adhered to the processes. There was key centralized ownership. Buy-in wasn't necessary because the same people that designed and implemented the processes were the same people that maintained them.

Building a Worldclass Infrastructure

We've heard this terminology from executives for the past several years. They all want to build a worldclass infrastructure. It sounds good, but what does it really mean? In this section we actually tell you what it is and show you how to implement it. Building that elusive worldclass infrastructure is a five-step process. If you implement the first four steps, congratulations, as you're three quarters of the way there! You're farther along than the 40 companies with which we performed case studies and probably 95 percent of the IT organizations out there.

The fifth step is to implement all the processes outlined in Table 5–1. But realistically speaking, in today's ultra-fast-paced world of technology advancement and limited resources, be content with implementing the first four steps. At least do that much and maybe the sequel to this book will be case studies on the IT infrastructures that made it.

Our list of characteristics for a worldclass infrastructure:

- High customer satisfaction
- Cost effective
- Data integrity (e.g., tape backups validated)
- Effective processes
- Good communication practices (internal and external to IT)

- Well established metrics
- Practiced disaster recovery process
- Cost of services are well documented
- Ability to benchmark services
- High RAS

A bit much to swallow? Now be honest with us. How many client/server environments have those ingredients?

Worldclass is nothing more than just another term for RAS. But we all like new things. How do you achieve it?

Start Simple

The preceding list of characteristics depicts the ultimate computing environment for IT and the corporation. To get there is a long and tedious ordeal. It's an evolutionary process that could take up to two years. But you need to start somewhere. If you take it all on you will surely fail. We list the steps in prioritized order, and you should not deviate from this sequence.

After the second step we recommend that you take on step three as soon as possible. We ask that you start by implementing or fixing the three most critical processes only to get some successes under your belt before taking on the entire scope outlined in Table 4–1—please, no more or less to start than with the three most critical processes in IT:

- Change control
- Problem management
- Client/Server production acceptance

All are critical. There really is no way to prioritize them. Depending on the size of your shop, it could take six months to a year to complete this step. But these are the minimum requirements to building that elusive worldclass infrastructure. You cannot wait any longer.

The fourth step is the whole enchilada. It's documenting your services, implementing metrics, and benchmarking your services.

The fifth step is the icing on the cake. Chances are that very few will ever take on this step, but if you have plenty of time and resources, then go for it!

The Simple Five-Step Program

We in IT have been trying to take on too much at one time. As we said earlier, the infrastructure is so far behind that it would be futile and a sure formula for failure to take on everything at one time. Start simple! Follow the five-step process that follows and you will succeed.

Building a worldclass infrastructure is a five-step process. Table 7–1 highlights the process:

Table 7–1   The Five Steps to Building a Worldclass Infrastructure

Step	Process
One	One-to-two day infrastructure assessment
Two	Organizational analysis and restructuring
Three	Establish processes: ●Defining the scope of production ●Process design ●Implementation
Four	●Establish metrics ●Documenting services ●Benchmarking services ●Marketing and selling services
Five	Implementing remaining processes in Table 5–1

Step 1

The first step is information gathering that is our one- to two-day assessment process. An outside consultant (see Appendix A for the program) should perform the appraisal.

Step 2

The second step will always be a detailed organizational analysis and restructure. Notice that we said "always." Remember 40 of 40—that's

100 percent—companies had organizational issues with which to contend. The interviewee doesn't say that, but many of the issues he or she brings up always point back to the organization.

The process is quite simple (see Table 7–2). Our role is that of the facilitator. We guide and mentor the team.

Table 7–2   Organizational Analysis and Restructure Process

Process	Duration
Management meetings to understand the current organization, business issues, political atmosphere and some of the key players. We also discuss the process of this organization assessment and restructure.	4 hours
Management gathers at an offsite location to share IT goals, initiatives, and functional responsibilities. Then the group holds discussions on restructuring the organization to resolve top issues from the 1 to 2 day high-level infrastructure assessment. The offsite agenda will be to: • Communicate the process and the objectives of this organization assessment. • Review most common problems in the industry today. • Take a closer look at the companies (case studies) involved in these 1 to 2 day assessments. • Present issues uncovered by the initial assessment. • Identify details of the current organization, its history and evolution. • Identify business issues and initiatives. • Understand political atmosphere. • Identify functional responsibilities. • Work with the group to organize and prioritize their issues and outline a detailed plan to execute changes. • Restructure the organization.	2 days
Technical staff gathers at an offsite meeting to understand functional responsibilities. The purpose is to discuss key issues and map out a new organization structure that tackles the issues and prepares for future initiatives. The offsite agenda will be the same as above.	1 to 2 days
Meet with management to compare notes from technical session.	2 hours
Interview key personnel to acquire additional data if required.	1 to 2 days
Assemble report.	5 to 8 days
Present findings to senior executive.	2 to 4 hours

Step 3

Step 3 is the very important process design and implementation. But before you can implement processes you need to define your scope of production (see our book titled *Building the New Enterprise* for a detailed explanation of how to define the scope of production). Once identified, design and implement no more than three of the processes outlined in Step 3 that are missing. We say only three because you need to get these right. The infrastructure review highlights the most critical processes to implement and usually the most comprehensive. Get these right first.

Step 4

Step 4 is designing and implementing metrics, documenting services, costing services and benchmarking the services with external sources (i.e., vendors, competitors, etc.). See Chapters 8 and 9 of *Building the New Enterprise*.

Step 5

The fifth step is to implement the rest of the processes in Table 5–1. As of August 1999, the 40 companies we studied did not have the first four steps implemented. Step 5 is what we refer to as icing on the cake. If you get this far, please e-mail us.

Designing and Adhering to Your Key Methodologies

The first step in resolving the many issues highlighted earlier in Table 2–1 and building a worldclass infrastructure is to establish the right methodologies to support a mission-critical production environment. The following are what we believe to be the most important 13 commandments:

1. Thy network should be thy data center.

Ask yourself: What is the most secure and reliable environment in data processing? Every IT professional can answer that one! The data center! It's your company's security blanket for essential, mission-critical, bread-and-butter applications such as financial, manufacturing, and HR business systems.

We can hear those desktop cowboys stirring right now. Yes, there are some desktop applications that could be considered mission-critical. And with client/server the desktop has become more important. But we agree only to a point. Desktops do not form the central nervous system of major organizations. If a desktop goes down, or even a LAN becomes unavailable, if a company will survive. Certainly a few people will take an unplanned break, but the WAN will keep the rest of the company actively employed. However, the desktop, file and print servers, and LANs are becoming as important, and in some cases more important, than the business applications. In this vein, the data center processes become more important when considering the whole enterprise.

As you deploy the proper infrastructure, your objective should be to make the network as reliable, available, and serviceable as the data center. This requires processes, standards, and procedures (discipline).

2. Thou must organize thy enterprise to support mission-critical, not technology.

Restructuring the organization to support networked client/server computing is the most important and critical aspect to implementing RAS. This book's primary focus is on the many organizational issues with today's client/server computing environments. If the organization is structured properly, then processes can flourish and RAS will be attainable.

The secret to properly structuring the organization is to focus on mission-critical support, not the technology. Split your infrastructure support organization into two parts: mission-critical and non-mission-critical. Once this is accomplished, then establish three levels of support for your mission-critical environment and implement a production control function. Even in today's networked-crazed world, when most people think of mission critical they associate it with mainframe computing because it was synonymous with mainframe computing. In the seventies and eighties MIS didn't focus on the technology. The focus was on supporting the enterprise's bread-and-butter applications 24 hours a day and seven days a week.

3. Thou shall maintain centralized control with decentralized operations.

Implement the new enterprise with a mixture of centralized control and decentralized operations. Centralized control means controlling costs, developing architectures, and deploying standards from a central location. Just as critical, key processes require centralized ownership.

Decentralized operations means it doesn't matter where your IT support personnel are located. They can be placed to best support networked computing in general and your customer specifically.

4. Honor thy mainframe disciplines and keep them holy, but keep out the bureaucracy.

Whether your company has a mainframe environment or not, it is crucial to understand the importance of mainframe disciplines, processes and procedures, standards, and guidelines—we can't live with them and can't live without them. In the age of distributed everything to everywhere, disciplines are more important than ever. But you cannot simply transplant mainframe disciplines with all their bureaucracy on client/server technology. You need to customize and streamline these disciplines so they can manage a modern, chaotic, heterogeneous infrastructure. We grew up with these processes in the legacy environment, which included change management, capacity planning, disaster recovery, and so on. Today, we need these disciplines more than ever—but not the bureaucracy.

5. Keep thy processes minimum yet sufficient.

Develop minimum yet sufficient enterprise-wide standards, processes, architectures, documentation, etc., for each area of the infrastructure, including the network, data center, desktops, development tools, nomadic computers, servers, and so on. You need standards for today, and clear statements of direction for your standards, environments, platforms, paradigms, or architectures (you pick the buzzword) for the future.

6. *Thou shall measure customer satisfaction!*

IT has abandoned the process of measuring customer satisfaction. The old process of sending out quarterly survey forms was ineffective. IT was lucky to receive 25 to 30 percent feedback. In today's hectic and crazy world, no one has the time to answer questions.

Design a new process with a point-and-click solution to measure every trouble ticket and work request submitted to the help desk. The goal is to achieve 100 percent feedback. It's doable!

7. *Keep all production systems equal in the eyes of the IT staff.*

From a hardware perspective, today's enterprise consists of mainframes, PCs, Macintoshes, workstations, servers, etc. You might be tempted to create separate support groups for each. Wrong! Now don't misunderstand us, you still need experts in different technologies, but providing an environment that promotes equal opportunity (the ability to easily cross-train) is critical.

Do not build silos surrounding technologies. Your support team should be referred to as technical support (no more and no less) and all its staff members should be cross-trained on as many platforms as each can handle.

Separating support along technologies results in inefficiencies, duplication of efforts (e.g., systems management tools), political issues, poor communications, and awful morale. These are a few problems that will occur when organizing to focus on a particular technology. Today, when everyone is doing more with less, you need to get the most out of your staff. Never reorganize based on technology.

8. *Measure all; verily, you cannot manage what you do not measure.*

Think back to the legacy environment and how they were able to measure every aspect of the infrastructure. Some of the metrics that we gathered included:

- Online system availability
- Network availability

- Number of trouble calls
- Number of application amendments
- Application response times
- Percentage of trouble calls resolved within specified time periods such as two hours, four hours, etc.

Ask any IT executive who was in MIS in the seventies and eighties about systems availability. They'll tell you they were proud to respond with 99.5 percent, 99.8 percent, and so on. What about today's networked enterprise? Forget it. Who has the time to collect all this trivia? We'll be the first to agree it takes energy to establish metrics. It took time, a lot of time, to collect uptime statistics in the mainframe era, but it was one of the reasons the legacy world was so reliable. We knew the numbers. We managed because we measured. Crunch your uptime numbers, hold people accountable, and your people will somehow find a way to run your shop more efficiently.

9. Build an attractive, cost-effective, and flexible service and thy customers will come back.

Once you get your house in order your customers will come back. But most IT shops are far from getting their internal workings in order. In the eighties, most of IT's customers abandoned the centralized support group to develop and deploy their own client/server applications. Centralized IT was too bureaucratic and costly.

Today, those same customers have felt the pain of trying to support their own mini-IT operations and, quite frankly, are willing to give up the technology-support issues. They need help, but centralized IT still must re-engineer itself to provide a better level of service.

Once processes are streamlined and cost efficient, your house (infrastructure) will support the New Enterprise. Then you need to advertise your services. Yes, services are what matters. People need business problems solved, not technology offerings to admire.

10. Thou shall market and sell thy infrastructure products to the customers.

In the olden days, mainframe staff would meditate in data centers perched in lofty ivory towers. The only time they would interact with common users is when the help desk would beckon with an unusual problem. We operated in reactionary mode.

Today, IT professionals need to walk with the great unwashed and communicate with customers. We need to schmooze, sell, and otherwise promote our services.

11. Thou shall develop thy proper curriculum and spend the time to properly transition and mentor the staff.

It's not about just sending your staff to technical training classes. It's about establishing the proper curriculum with hands-on projects and assignments. You also need to keep your staff abreast of the latest widget and gadget—technology is changing by the hour.

If you have a legacy staff, put your feet in their shoes. They've been doing the same things on the same platform for decades. Many of them can learn new technologies, and having their mission-critical data center mentality is invaluable.

12. Thou shall implement a cost-of-service methodology that's simple and inexpensive to maintain.

You need to be on your toes at all times. Implementing a cost-of-service methodology is critical, not for your customer, but for IT. You need to:

- Identify your services.
- Document the cost of those services.
- Benchmark your infrastructure against external competition.

Once you get your house in order, provide menus to your customers outlining services, the charges associated with those services, and that of external competition. Beat them to the punch. They're always knocking IT for being too expensive and providing lousy service—"I can go out and find it elsewhere with much better results." Hey, words are easy. Like we said, beat them to the punch!

13. Honor thy users and communicate with them often via a process.

Don't just talk about improving communication. Don't rely on monthly or quarterly get-togethers. Networked computing has destroyed whatever little communication there was between IT and its users and internally within IT. There must be a process that promotes and instills effective communication practices on a daily basis.

Know That Success Equals the Change You Manage

Change will not stop. In fact, we are all now running on Internet time, even if our companies do not sell products that operate on any network. Technology is evolving and shifting faster than ever. Follow the first thirteen methodologies in building a worldclass infrastructure and you will find success.

The New Order

In this chapter we discuss how client/server computing is changing the IT department. We discuss the technology and roles that each group now needs to play in this new world.

Client/server technology has changed many relationships within the IT department. The distribution of power is shifting because of the need for team development and deployment of client/server information systems. a team approach that we didn't experience during the mainframe days. How will this redistribution of power change the information technology infrastructure and alter the IT organizational structure? The answers require a rethinking of the distribution of responsibilities.

We started this book by discussing the common problems we found among the 40+ organizations that we studied. We discussed the importance of an infrastructure reminiscent of mainframe days, an infrastructure that is reliable, available, and serviceable. The problem in attaining this RAS environment is the politics that accompany any redistribution of organizational power.

Now let's talk the politics of client/server. Politics you say! Yes, the use of client/server technology has caused IT departments great pains. Internal politics have resulted in the altering of the logical arrangement of IT resources within the department. For example, most IT departments began their foray into the client/server world by creating a separate and distinct applications programming group. They purchased a server, application development tools, and most likely a database engine. Using these tools, they created a local area network and isolated themselves from the network backbone. Ironically, many IT departments treated these groups in the same way that the PC pioneers were treated.

Once the client/server group established its own world within the IT department, it proceeded to establish its own change management process or, in some cases, eliminate the process altogether. The client/server group created the first application and took control and ownership of the installation. In most cases technical support (server administration), network support, and desktop support turned the installation keys over to the client/server group. This left the group with the impression that it could continue down a road separate from the established infrastructure.

This may sound familiar and may have even occurred in your IT department. This set of events unfortunately may just have made the job of integrating the client/server group with the rest of the IT department a difficult and tedious effort.

Autonomous client/server groups that we observed liked being autonomous. They liked having their own rules. They liked not being part of the bureaucratic world of the mainframe-dominated IT department. What is really ironic is that many of the mainframe support groups didn't want the client/server information systems to leave the control and domain of the client/server group. The IT department establishment knew that once the information systems transferred technical support ownership, they were responsible (a responsibility that many of the mainframe staff didn't want).

So, how do we bring the two groups together? How do we bring the disciplines of the mainframe RAS environments to the client/server world? First, we need to decide the demarcation of technologies and the corresponding group that will build or support them. Yes, we know that client/server information systems development often requires desktop, network, database, and development tool knowledge, but this group can't do it all, not if you truly want RAS and an integrated information systems environment.

Splitting the Technologies

In the mainframe-only world, each information systems subgroup (e.g., applications, technical support, etc.) handled its respective technical responsibilities in a coordinated manner, but the system and application software were designed to run basically separate from each other. The integration between the application layer and the system software layer was designed to be hierarchical, such as by permitting the applications group to develop programs and pass the source code to the production environment for compilation. System administration was not a concern for the applications programmer. This is not true in the client/server world.

Client/server technology is divided into three layers: presentation layer, business-code layer, and data layer. The presentation layer's purpose is to manage user-interface functions such as mouse clicks, scroll bars, and the visual layout. The business-code layer is the middle tier, and its purpose is to enforce business rules through programmable constructs such as requiring that purchase orders must reference a vendor. This is where the algorithms execute and the general data manipulation occurs. Layer three is the data or database tier. The purpose of this layer is to manage data storage and retrieval such as storing a record or executing a query. Now, depending on the type of client/server configuration you are deploying, the layer's basic function may be enhanced to also perform additional activities. For instance, there are light clients, light servers, heavy clients, and heavy servers. The general direction today is towards light clients and heavy servers because of the dramatic growth of the Internet and Web-based programming. The major software companies (SAP, Oracle, Peoplesoft, etc.) are all transitioning to light clients and heavy servers using a three-tier architecture.

What is a three-tier architecture? Well, client/server comes in two basic configurations, two-tier and three-tier. Two-tier client/server uses a presentation layer and a data layer, and places the process code either on the client or the server. Three-tier client/server splits the presentation, process, and data layers on separate computing complexes. In some deployments of three-tier, multiple process and data servers are used to permit linear growth. Therefore, utilizing cheaper personal computer complexes provides similar performance compared to what the traditional mainframe offered, as the end user on a PC or Macintosh uses a Web browser to matriculate the application. In this sense the end user's PC acts somewhat like a dumb terminal. A traditional mainframe environment was like a one-tier architecture, although there was a separation of the presentation, process, and data layers. The difference is that all three layers executed on the same computing complex.

The client/server environment introduces new challenges and coordination issues. We now have many computing complexes to manage. The desktop and server may be cheaper, but the complexity of many computing complexes interacting in the multi-protocol network is difficult to manage. A client/server environment requires that we share resources on the desktop and the server. Yes, we shared resources on the mainframe, but there was a clearer delineation of software responsibilities. The natural hierarchy of the mainframe separated the application from the system software. An information systems department using Cobol for its application software language rarely needed to address memory conflicts caused by application software. Products such as CICS from IBM handled this for the applications programmer. In the client/server world, desktop conflicts are common more often than we would like.

So, we are beginning to see the first issue. How do we build information systems that use multiple computers and divide up the ownership and management of each layer (presentation, process, and data)? Second, who is ultimately responsible for the desktops, the process servers, and the data servers? Third, what are the rules of engagement that will permit the various groups that will touch the desktop and servers to coexist?

These are not simple questions and there are no easy solutions. This is were the politics begin and were the politics can kill an IT department.

Who's in Charge?

The separation of information systems layers lends itself to the division of the organizational responsibilities. It also may lead to the reorganization of the IT department. Management of each layer is a critical component of the client/server success and many existing IT organizational structures do not permit a clear management role over specific layers. For example, the systems support group manages mainframe teleprocessing software and the applications-programming group programs the applications software written to run under the teleprocessing software's control. This is a clear delineation of responsibilities and roles.

In the client/server environment, it is not clear who has management control over the desktop environment. Does desktop support, applications, or network administration manage the desktop and administer change management? Most information systems departments permit different groups to manage the desktop as needed. Servers are a different story and management is usually divided among server administration, network administration, and database administration. The applications development group normally doesn't need to get involved with the management of the servers.

Some clarification is needed about group names. Traditional IBM-type mainframe IT departments consisted of systems support (network and operation systems), database support, operations support, and application support. IT departments supporting client/server or networked heterogeneous hardware and software (mainframes, minis, PCs, and client/server) environments look a lot different.

During the transitional phase, the mainframe IT department retained the existing organization structure and created the separate client/server minigroup. In essence, the client/server group was viewed as another sub-part of the mainframe IT department. The growth of client/server caused the evolution of the IT department to address the management of the layers and who should be responsible for each layer.

Many IT organizations that have mature client/server systems use this formula for layer management. The systems support group manages all servers and network connections including network interface cards (NICs) and the associated network software. Database administration manages the database software, desktop support manages the desktop operating system software, and the applications group manages customer software requests. It doesn't seem like a big organizational change, but it is. Network administration cannot load software or change configuration settings without desktop support's knowledge and concurrence.

Teamwork and cooperation thus become extremely important. The desktop support group just became a team of highly skilled technicians on the same level as network administration, server administration, and database administration. In the mainframe world, systems support applied changes to the teleprocessing software and applications development was generally unaware. Network administration of the systems support area cannot apply changes to desktop configurations without the knowledge of the product's deployment team.

The product deployment team is a group that has overall management of the information systems. Members include representatives from each functional area and management is done by consensus. This is a radical shift for many information systems departments. Each member of the team is responsible for his or her specific area and the team must reach consensus on disputed issues. The rules of engagement have changed. Team consensus is necessary for client/server information systems to succeed. The IT organization must be structured to enable effective consensus.

The Organization for the Twenty-First Century

Whether it's the twenty-first or thirtieth century, whether it's legacy computing, client/server computing or something new coming along in the next N number of years, if you're supporting mission-critical systems, don't tamper with something that's worked for several decades. As we mentioned earlier in the book, mission critical in the IT world is synonymous with mainframe computing, Please don't let mainframe computing turn you off. Keep an open mind as you read this section. Much of what we discuss evolved from the nasty mainframe era.

In our 1994 book, *Rightsizing the New Enterprise*, we made a comment which we still use at speaking engagements, "Don't trash mainframe disciplines." In 1994 we were referring to processes. After performing extensive case studies we include the organization structure in the category of mainframe disciplines. Don't trash the disciplines!

In this section we introduce you to the structure to best support Enterprise Computing. Not mainframe computing, not client/server computing, but Enterprise Computing. Technology has nothing to do with it.

You'll probably go into shock after reading the first few paragraphs of this section. After 40 infrastructure assessments encompassing hundreds of pages of data, history repeats itself.

We started putting together a structure to resolve the issues shown in Table 2–1 and, lo and behold, it looked very familiar. Much of the structure looked just like the mainframe data center environment that evolved back in the 1970s.

We kept doubting our overall solution. After all, how would it look to be part of the Enterprise Computing Institute and sound like mainframe people? Is it a coincidence? Actually, the more you think about it, the more it makes sense. No other environment provided better RAS for supporting mission-critical applications than the mainframe environment. The key words are mission-critical. Technology had absolutely nothing to do with it. So why did we choose to ignore it after all these years? We automatically assumed that it wouldn't work for client/server computing because the technology and architecture was so much different. And let's not forget the bad rap the mainframe environment received in the late eighties and early nineties. But as we enter the 21st century, IT professionals better wake up and start embracing the positive aspect from that era!

We need to stop the rhetoric and stop reinventing the wheel. A good example of this is how companies with non-mainframe environments do everything possible *not* to use the term data center. In our travels we've heard that the term data center has a mainframe connotation. So what's the point? They refer to it as the production server room, Server room, computer room, etc. Come on gang, let's really be proud of what the data center exemplified.

Enterprise Services

We like referring to the infrastructure group as Enterprise Services. It has a nice ring to it for the twenty-first century. The organization chart in Figure 9–1 represents the infrastructure support and development organization of the future.

We included first-, second-, and third-level support roles for each of the areas. We highlight this in the organization chart in Figure 9–1 because it's one of the most critical of the functions that were abandoned as we transitioned to client/server, and it happens to be one of the biggest reasons RAS for client/server doesn't exist.

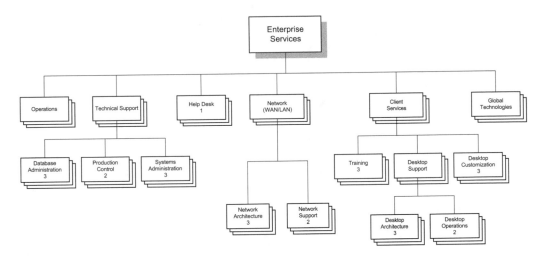

Figure 9–1 Infrastructure support and development organization of the future.

Mission-Critical vs. Non-Mission-Critical

After reviewing the data it became apparent that we needed to separate the infrastructure between mission-critical (24×7) and non-mission-critical (9×5) support. Always a controversial subject, but necessary to do. Controversial because people will argue that in the client/server world the desktop is just as critical as those big data center servers housing the applications or database. We happen to agree. This is where we need to put this to bed once and for all. If a mission-critical server goes down, it affects hundreds and sometimes thousands of users, but should a single desktop or even a LAN go down, some people might be inconvenienced for a while, but it won't break the bank. Those enterprise systems for HR, manufacturing, etc., are mission-critical. Systems requiring around-the-clock support need to be branded mission-critical. Mission-critical support needs critical processes that require a specialized group like production control to implement and maintain them.

The 24×7 group is paid not to sleep. Their life should evolve around the infrastructure. When a server goes down, the on-call support staff jumps. The 9×5 group is equally as important but is not on call twenty-four hours a day/seven days a week. The specificity of mission-critical will vary from company to company. For example, some businesses may require 24×7 support for e-mail.

Structuring Technical Staff

All staff supporting mission-critical systems within Enterprise Services should be structured in the same manner with two levels of support: junior technicians (second-level support personnel) working very closely with senior technicians (third-level support staff) and reporting into the same management. This allows for:

- Second-level or junior- technical personnel to accelerate employee skill development.
- Second-level technical personnel to have a clearly-defined career path.
- Improved communication between second- and third-level support. They'll be working on implementing projects and production support issues together.
- Discussing projects and support issues in the same staff meetings.
- Second- and third-level technical support personnel will have the same group goals and objectives.
- Improved turnaround for problem resolution.
- Freed senior staff to provide analysis on new technologies, and fully implement and customize system management tools. It also allows the time for senior technical staff to architect the proper infrastructure.
- Second-level technical personnel to implement and maintain system management tools alongside the senior staff.
- Second-level personnel not designated as "support only." They need to be working on projects together with senior technicians.

Second- and third-level technical staff should be physically located in the same area. They should be having coffee breaks together and attending technical support group outings. There cannot be any organizational barriers.

Functional Responsibilities

Enterprise Services

Enterprise Services is the infrastructure design, architecture, development, and production support organization for the 21st century.

Enterprise Services supports and maintains the client/server hardware and software, including the distributed servers and databases that are required for mission-critical applications. This means Enterprise Services is responsible for everything from security to backups, disaster recovery to change control. Enterprise Services personnel also regularly schedule and run production jobs that update databases and download data to distributed processing. They also support the development of new business-system processing applications.

Reliability, availability, and serviceability is the key responsibility of Enterprise Services. Sure, every group within IT is involved with RAS, but someone needs to own RAS! This responsibility translates into several stages of support, starting with the RAS services which include hardware and software maintenance, processing control for managing disk and tape storage media, systems security, and access controls over networks and data. Among other things, Enterprise Services is responsible for maintaining online access (security, performance, and availability) and capacity planning. The sections that follow portray the five main groups and some of the responsibilities that fall under Enterprise Services. The five groups and subgroups we discuss are:

1. Technical Support
   - Database Administration
   - Systems Administration
   - Production Control
2. Operations
3. Help Desk
4. Network
   - Network Architecture
   - Network Support
5. Client Services

- Training
- Desktop Customization
- Desktop Support
- Desktop Architecture
- Desktop Operations

Technical Support

The first main group we need to look at is what we call Technical Support. Within Technical Support we divide production-computing tasks into three smaller groups: Database Administration, Systems Administration, and Production Control.

Technical Support has responsibility for the infrastructure development and production support functions. This group is also responsible for maintaining the operating systems, production databases and the development and implementation of systems administration and systems management software for all mission-critical computer platforms. The professionals in this group are the ones that design and implement the heart and soul of your infrastructure. Technical Support's charter is to perform systems management for an organization's mission-critical (24×7) production servers and, when needed, development servers. The group is responsible for providing a consistent, reliable environment thus ensuring maximum server uptime in support of maximum application availability in an efficient and cost-effective manner. Technical Support provides these services 24 hours a day, 365 days a year, with on-call support for servers in the production environment.

Among its services, Technical Support coordinates the preparation of new business applications and new releases to existing applications for use in a RAS-disciplined, production-computing environment (productionalization) according to the processes and procedures detailed in the Client/Server Production Acceptance (CSPA) process which was highlighted as a key process to implement. In fact, Technical Support acts as the main contact between CSPA project members and the rest of the IT infrastructure. Technical Support coordinates contact between IT and their business customers to ensure that the CSPA steps are followed and in the proper sequence. For instance, Technical Support assigns support staff to projects, sets up initial team meetings, distributes weekly status updates, and facilitates signoff of the completed CSPA by all involved parties.

Technical Support also works with customers to install, set up power, and connect the network to their production servers in the data center, as well as install associated peripherals (modems, for instance), and arrange a preventive maintenance check for all hardware coming into the data center. Once the equipment is in place, Technical Support then partitions the disks and installs the operating system on the servers. Technical Support applies patches and other modifications to the operating system, as necessary, and according to Technical Support standards and practices. Technical Support also installs and maintains the databases and database-management systems. Technical Support provides and maintains the various networking services, including information systems (NIS), distributed file systems (NFS), and domain-name services (DNS). Finally, Technical Support installs any third-party software products on the servers. Technical Support executes plans and processes to remove antiquated servers and applications from the production environment.

Database Administration Now let's take a look a closer look at Enterprise Services, the organization for the twenty-first century. The Database Administration group implements and supports the organization's databases, database management systems, and software in a manner that provides a highly reliable, available, and supportable production environment.

- Responsible for developing, implementing, and maintaining the database environment, including system and application software support.

- Responsible for planning and configuring the database environment.

- Evaluates and makes recommendations on purchase and utilization of software products.

- Performs installation and maintenance on database management systems.

- Performs problem diagnoses and determines resolution for application and system software.

- Coordinates and provides support to applications programmers, system programmers, users and computer operations personnel.

- Develops and maintains standards and procedures for the database environment.

- Measures database system performance and tunes where applicable.

- Installs and upgrades database management system software with new releases and maintenance releases. Upgrades to DBMS software will be coordinated with the applications support staff, when needed. Release-level consistency will be maintained across all affected/mod environments, support, staging, and production.

- Installs DBMS patches as supplied by the vendor as needed in coordination with Systems Administration and the applications support staff.

- Provides consultation support to Systems Administration regarding operating system release implementation.

- Provides 24 hours a day, seven days a week, 365 days a year, on-call support for production DBMS problem resolution.

- Responsible for design procedures for business continuation planning (i.e., backup and recovery) as required by system-availability agreements for each application.

- Responsible for verification and correction of errors on non-production status databases on an as-requested basis.

- Consults with application developers in designing security methodologies to establish end-user access to the database. The use of standard access methods for application-controlled access will be encouraged as appropriate.

- Provides problem resolution support for DBMS application related errors.

- Supports impact analysis activity related to application design and modification.

- Provides consultation for system configuration of new applications, such as use of raw partitions vs. file system, client/server architecture.

- Provides consultation for selection of the DBMS.

- Enforces conformance to database and data center standards in application systems prior to production implementation.

- Provides consultation and development support for the physical database design for database applications in production and development environments.

- Provides consultation support for logical database design for database applications in production and development environments.

- Acts as interface with DBMS software vendors and other internal support groups (e.g., Sybase contact).

- Responsible for physical integrity of the production databases which includes regularly-scheduled verification procedures and correction of errors.

- Provides problem resolution support for DBMS-related errors.

- Responsible for monitoring database user access.

- Responsible for monitoring physical capacity.

- Responsible for database performance tuning.

- Responsible for maintaining and providing DBA level access as required for all production status applications on production and support/staging environments. DBA level access in a development environment will be shared with the development staff.

- Monitors informational/error logs for messages specific to system operation. Responsibility for monitoring will be shared with applications support and security administration.

- Assists applications support staff in providing device configuration data (hardware and software) for Systems Administration, such as disk usage, memory, etc.

- Maintains system runtime configuration information to define the DBMS's execution.

- Performs database modification function against production applications, such as alter table. Support for non-production status applications will be as requested by the support staff.

- Provides database support for disaster recovery in conjunction with systems programming.

Systems Administration Systems Administration is your highly skilled 24×7 mission-critical, production-support function. This is also the group that designs and architects the heart and soul of your infrastructure.

- Measures systems and network performance and recommends and implements performance improvements.

- Evaluates new products and recommends updates and upgrades.

- Performs capacity-planning studies and identifies capacity shortages.

- Supports mission-critical business systems by providing reliable system software, including operating systems and associated applications.

- Diagnoses and resolves unique and most complex systems problems.

- Installs related program products and support tools.

- Designs configuration management.

- Develops standards.

- Architects and designs the infrastructure.

- Designs and participates in a disaster recovery process.

Production Control The third Technical Support group is Production Control (operations analysts or entry-level system administrators) which acts as technical liaison among the programming staff, user community, data base administrators, systems administrators, and computer operations to resolve production problems, implement new systems, and make changes to existing systems.

The natural migration for an operations analyst is to become a second-level or senior systems administrator. Senior systems administrators rely heavily on the operations analysts to assist on every project. Second-level problem determination is also handled by Production Control, with escalation to a systems administrator if required.

- Assures Production QA.

- Has ownership of Change Control.

- Has ownership of the Client/Server Production Acceptance (CSPA) Process.

- Provides second-level System Administration support.

- Administers Disk Management.

- Participates in Disaster Recovery (process & drills).

- Maintains and Customizes System Management Tools.

- Maintains Server Inventory.

- Maintains scheduling requirements.

Operations

The Operations group supports the production-computing environment. This group ensures cost-effective use of data center resources, timely response for system failures, and is tasked to provide maximum effectiveness in routine, daily operations.

- Operators monitor the network and all production servers on the network.

- Operators perform daily incremental (changed files only) and weekly (full) backups of all file systems in the data center. They also clean tape drives, prepare labels (server names) for hardware and follow problem management procedures to contact proper support personnel in response to users' problems.

- The tape librarian's function is responsible for electronic and external tape labels and bar codes, and coordinates with an off-site vendor to safely store backup tapes and restore files as required.

- Allocates space, including maintaining an equipment location map and installing the console, network, and power connections for new servers. Operations are expected to routinely evaluate resource capabilities and anticipate future requirements.

- Runs diagnostic tests to detect machine malfunctions.

- Monitors daily, weekly, and monthly batch processing.

- Responsible for the coordination and proper execution of special processing requirements.

- Maintains data center facilities.

- Maintains system hardware and software and contributes toward the resolution of problems.

- Provides detailed recommendations for policies, procedures, and guidelines and assists in their generation and implementation.

- Works with IT technical staff and vendors to efficiently resolve problems and restart the systems.

- Monitors control panels, magnetic tape units, and other off-line equipment.

- Maintains physical plant and support systems (power, cooling, etc.). This also includes uninterrupted maintenance services despite weather, utility problems, or disasters, security for equipment and data, and fire detection and suppression systems, not to mention the many contingency plans to quickly restore operations following a disaster.

The Help Desk

The Help Desk has not changed over the years. Its primary responsibility is first-level problem resolution. The Help Desk provides a central point of contact for customer help, problem status, and feedback to customers. An employee in this position is the focal point for reporting problems and minor system problem resolutions including monitoring of data communications, on-line applications, and large complex network systems on a variety of hardware platforms. Work is evaluated based on quality of results obtained, conferences, feedback from customers, and reports.

- Ownership of global problem management.

- Responsible for user administration, passwords, user adds/deletes, software administration, database IDs, access rights, Internet e-mail IDs.

- Answers Help Desk telephones and uses first-level problem determination techniques to analyze and solve problems.

- Interfaces with internal staff, external service providers, and customers to facilitate timely resolution of all reported problems.

- Performs system availability verification procedures to ensure service-level requirements.

- Initiates recovery procedures for terminals, printers, modems, controllers, and all telecommunications devices.

- Maintains contact with all customers until a problem has been resolved and informs them of current status.

- Provides recommendations to problem and change regarding any configuration, problem, or change concern.

- Provides electronic mail support.

Network

The network is the most critical piece of the infrastructure as it relates to client/server computing. The network group is split into two sub-groups: Architecture and Support. They manage the development of communications, networking, and systems standards and policies for connected computing environments. They also manage the development and implementation of company-wide short- and long-range data communications, networking strategies and deployment plans.

Network Architecture The professionals responsible for Network Architecture are in charge of the planning and design of the network and for coordinating network functions. They are responsible for technical support of the network, including planning, implementation and operational support. The group is responsible for technical consulting and systems design for implementation, management, and operational support of information network communication systems.

The functions for the Network Architecture group include:

- Defines network requirements.

- Develops network strategies, plans, and designs.

- Evaluates new network technologies.

- Develops and implements network standards and procedures.

- Ensures there is adequate network capacity.

- Tests new network technologies.

- Manages network configuration, names, and addresses.

- Configures and installs inter-network devices like routers and gateways.

- Analyzes complex problems and coordinates resolutions.

- Performs communication and networking systems analysis and design planning for integration of computer systems into a local/ wide area network based upon business analysis research.

- Evaluates customer requests or projects, analyzes requirements and pertinent technical information, then develops and implements quality, cost-effective solutions.

- Installs, customizes and tests network communications and desktop workstation systems.

- Evaluates enterprise networking components and infrastructure, develops detailed analysis reports and recommendations for network and data communications systems.

- Performs communication and networking systems quality analysis of integrated computer systems into a local/wide area network(s).

- Analyzes and participates in the development of security standardization and implementation of security controls for local and wide area networks.

- Participates in the development and enforcement of communications and networking systems, and desktop workstation standards and policies for connected computing environments.

- Participates in the development and implementation of company-wide short- and long-range data communications and enterprise networking strategies.

- Assists in preparing budgets for data communications systems and desktop workstations.

- Coordinates system changes with appropriate support staff to ensure uninterrupted computer services to the affected Enterprise departments and responsible executives.

Network Support The responsibility for implementation and operations of the network lies with the Network Support group. These professionals are responsible for planning, implementing, and coordinating the installation, enhancement or operational support of simple and advanced information network systems and desktop workstations.

- Configures and installs data communications equipment.

- Acts as initial point of contact for network problems.

- Configures and installs concentrators.

- Connects desktop systems to the network.

- Maintains and documents the structured cabling system.

- Implements network standards and procedures.

- Monitors and reports network problems.

- Maintains inventory of spare equipment.

- Maintains purchase orders and maintenance agreements.

- Interfaces closely with other operations staff.

- Evaluates customer requests or project tasks, analyzes requirements and pertinent technical information, then develops and implements quality, cost-effective solutions.

- Installs, customizes, and tests network communications and desktop workstation systems.

- Monitors current network and computer system configurations and performance, creates technical reports, recommendations and solutions to meet short- and long-range goals.

- Provides operational and technical support of advanced information network hardware and software.

- Maintains inventory-control system and network-connection inventory to ensure proper asset management.

- Coordinates system changes with appropriate support staff to ensure uninterrupted computer services.

- Analyzes and participates in the development of security standardization and implementation of security controls for local and wide area networks.

- Participates in the development and enforcement of networking systems and desktop workstation standards and policies for connected computing environments.

- Reviews problem reporting and customer request systems and updates status or resolution text with current information.

- Keeps professional skills updated and consistent with current information systems networking technology and desktop workstations.

- Provides problem determination, repairs or upgrades to desktop workstations and peripheral devices at customer sites.

Client Services

The Client Services group is the 9×5 desktop-support group for which there are three main functions. Some organizations have a Training group so we've left it in. We've also included Customization and Desktop Support groups.

Training Those chartered with this responsibility handle professional work planning and deliver software training programs. Responsibilities include meeting training needs through individual and group instruction for standard office-automation software such electronic mail, as well as programs and/or systems developed by internal staff. Preparation of course outline, training schedules, training aids and course handouts are required.

- Develops course outlines, visual aids, and end user handouts for training classes offered.

- Participates in the evaluation and determination of standard office automation software products.

- Receives and processes training requests.

- Schedules training classes to ensure adequate levels of response to customer requests.

- Evaluates effectiveness of courses and makes changes as needed.

- Learns new and/or revised software applications to provide training as required.

- Develops useful documentation to support instruction given.

- Researches new products to assess and recommend adequate support levels.

- Receives training in developed applications to allow support in the customer environment.

- Maintains student history of classes attended.

Desktop Customization Desktop customization provides services that deal specifically with end-user productivity tools. The main support issue for the Desktop Customization group is the development of end-user systems and ensuring that documentation of user-built systems is recorded.

- Software implementation.

- Requirements analysis.

- End-user development management.

- Desktop development.

Desktop Support We divide Desktop Support in the same manner as we did for Technical Support under Enterprise Services. The architecture function looks at the latest and greatest hardware and software technologies and provides third-level support. Desktop Operations provides process ownership and second-level support

Desktop Architecture The Desktop Architecture function provides for the continued growth of the organization. This area concentrates on desktop unit management as well as technology direction. Inventory management is a critical activity of this group.

- Capacity planning

- Software distribution

- Testing

- Interoperability

- Roll-out plan

- Documentation

- Architecture

- Configuration management

- Peripherals support

- PC maintenance

- Standards

- Application standards

- Viruses

- Hardware installs

- Remote desktop

- Level 3 support for unique and complex problems

- Productivity tools

- Training

- Performance and tuning

- Desktop analysis

- Automation

Desktop Operations Desktop Operations provides daily support to all desktop customers. This is a labor-intensive job.

- Desktop patrol

- Hardware and software installs

- Level two support and troubleshooting

- Implements software distribution roll-out

- Maintains inventory

- Remote customer support (telecommuting)

- Telecommuting installs

Project Management

There is no getting around it. If you have a large IT department and plan to deploy client/server, then project management is a must. The biggest problem that we saw in our travels was that many well-conceived projects were late or cancelled because team members couldn't get together at the appropriate time. You know the scenario; everyone agrees to work together and three months down the line they are off on other projects. Sometimes this is unavoidable, but usually it is the result of management's lack of real resource information.

It is not uncommon for the same person to be scheduled on the same day to work on two or three different tasks. Once the employee informs the project management team that they cannot work on that task on that day, there is the possibility of a ripple effect of delays throughout the project. This is not unique. This situation will occur many times during the project and the end result is a project that is late, over budget, or the specifications are reduced to fit the budget and time frame.

Cross-Functional Teams

Cross-functional teams play a major role in the success of network computing. Since network computing incorporates so many pieces of the information technology arsenal, it is imperative that the functional areas of the technical expertise work together. This may seem obvious, but as we stated, many organizations separate technical talent based on different management decisions.

Network computing requires cross-functional teams for the technology to be successful. The real question is how to get the separate technical areas to work together and share knowledge. This is a cultural issue and is truly different for each organization.

1. We suggest unifying the management team. This is not a difficult task. Gather them all in the same room and talk about the project and value it will have for the organization. Continue this type of meeting to ensure that the importance of the project stays fresh in their minds.
2. Clearly define the technical roles and responsibilities for each team member.
3. Define the method of measurement and reward for each team member as it relates to the project.
4. Ensure that no employee is assigned to multiple activities on the same day. Don't multi-task your employees! It is bad for the project.
5. Teach your employees that sharing skills and knowledge is good and will be rewarded.

Once you have planned all this out, use cross-functional teams everywhere you can. They really work!

The "Worldclass" Infrastructure

As we spent time with each organization we began to see a common thread. Each organization was interested in network computing for the true value it would bring to the bottom line. Technology change was not just a thing to do to keep up with the Joneses, but rather a business requirement to stay competitive in a respective industry.

So how does a worldclass infrastructure add value? It adds value because it opens the door to opportunities that may not have been available. The power and promise of network computing is multimedia, access anytime, anywhere, and access to all corporate data. It's like paving a road where no road existed before and sitting back and watching what grows up around the road.

Organizations that build worldclass infrastructures find that they can do more than the competition and do it in shorter time periods. This gives them competitive advantage over their rivals.

Just look at the leading companies in most any field of business today—whether it be Wal-Mart, Federal Express or Sun Microsystems—these companies compete because they have built worldclass infrastructures. They win because they use their worldclass infrastructure to run the business more effectively and more efficiently, and it also brings them closer to their customers. Their metrics are better than their competitors.

The recent surge in application software that unifies the organization is a case in point. Enterprise resource planning and supply chain manage-

123

ment applications demand that the flow of data through the organization is fast and the data pure. The process is such that the data be entered once and appended as it flows through the various operations. This requires that the infrastructure permit the free flow of data from one platform to another. The days of silo information systems and isolated data networks are gone. The days of multiple data storage methods that do not permit retrieval of data as needed are gone. The days of redundant data with multiple versions of the data, are gone.

The worldclass infrastructure brings the organization and its customers together. It is the foundation for the future.

Appendix

Frequently-Asked Questions

As we travel the globe the questions keep pouring in. As we do with most of the books in the series, we've documented the most-commonly-asked questions as they pertain to this subject matter. This section is divided into the categories of people, process, and technology. We also included a section labeled general as some questions span multiple categories.

General

Q1. Why can't RAS flourish in client/server computing?

Client/server computing is like no other paradigm ever before in the history of computing. RAS will never flourish in this environment unless major focus is put on the proper design of the infrastructure. This means restructuring the organization and implementing a few very critical processes. And you need to implement metrics. We refer to it as building a world-class infrastructure. (See Chapter 7, Building a World-Class Infrastructure.)

Q2. Our IT shop is always in a reactive mode—how do we get out of this situation?

Every shop on the list of elite 40 was in a reactive mode with the same daily firefighting routine (in particular the System Administration staff). There was never any time for planning, system architecture, or analysis of new technology. We found that the cause of the reactive mode was a lack of predetermined, well-conceived processes, and infrastructure to support the people tasked with implementing them. In other words, there wasn't any proactive work done up front.

You can get out of this situation by structuring to focus on mission critical and not technology, implementing three levels of support, and setting up the processes and procedures outlined in our books *Rightsizing the New Enterprise, Managing the New Enterprise, Networking the New Enterprise,* and *Building the New Enterprise.*

See also our 13 commandments in Chapter 7, Building a World-Class Infrastructure. IT shops need to establish and follow a set of methodologies—a common set agreed upon by the entire organization.

Q3. Can IT ever become a company's competitive advantage?

Yes, but for now, as that ageless perception goes, IT is costing the company millions and what are the users getting in return? The CEO has no idea how much waste is really occurring in IT. Oh, they see the bottom line but they have no idea how much of that bottom figure is waste. We estimate that as much as 20 percent is waste—you add it up when most IT budgets are in the multi-million range. IT needs to get its house in order before it can ever expect to become a competitive advantage. IT will need to invest time and resource to building a world-class infrastructure.

Q4. How long will it take to build a world-class infrastructure?

The first four steps will take at least six months to a year to do it right, and possibly longer. The approach we provide you in this book is the quickest way of getting there. See Chapter 7 on how to build that elusive world-class infrastructure.

Q5. Management is always threatening to outsource the entire infrastructure or parts of the infrastructure. Is there anything we can do?

There's a lot you can do but it takes a lot of work. In this day and age you need to document your services, know the cost of these services, and be able to benchmark your services against vendors providing these types of services. You need to be one step ahead of management. If you do your homework and get your house in order, your costs should be lower than the competition. So much for the talk.

Q6. Why is it so difficult to draw lines of information technology demarcation in a network computing environment?

The main reason is the training and backgrounds of the IT employees. We call them Cowboys (client/server) and Dictators (mainframe) and they learned the IT business in very different environments. This causes great difficulty when you start discussing the separation of technical areas of responsibility that used to be owned by one or the other group. For example, deciding that the desktop should be the responsibility of the network group, or that database administration will control all databases on all platforms, is not easy for those that never aligned work responsibilities this way.

Q7. How does the information technology department truly provide local flexibility and centralized control?

This can really be a difficult one. We strongly recommend that in the areas of data management (i.e., backup and recovery), network backup support be made available in as many places as possible. Using tape backup silos and high bandwidth networks, overnight backups is a cost justifiable technology. Network management, server management, and software distribution management (either Web programs or application downloads) can provide behind-the-scene control with limited big brother image. A simple offering such as tape backup, disaster recovery storage for remote sites that insist that they must manage their systems, can be a major step forward to obtaining this goal.

Q8. Can the IT department deliver projects on time?

Yes. But it requires a different approach to project management and work in general. There is a method created by the Avraham Y. Goldratt Institute that manages projects in a very different and successful way. The basic premise is to work on one thing at a time, don't multi-task, and complete as many things in parallel as possible. We recommend that you view www.goldrattt.com for more information.

Q9. Is the IT department a support or strategic business function?

It is both in most organizational settings. The problem is that most organizations view the IT department as support, first and foremost. This can spell real disaster for an organization. Competitive advantage is more and more being defined by the use of information technology. Think strategic first, support second. The mind set change can do wonders for your organization.

People

Q1. How do you best structure the organization to support a networked heterogeneous environment?

This entire book focuses on just that. But if we were to highlight the most critical pieces of designing the proper organization, it would have to be designing three levels of support throughout your infrastructure, designing key centralized ownership of processes, and focusing on mission critical vs. non-mission critical.

Q2. We can't find enough technical resources? What do we do?

This will only get worse as we head into the twenty-first century. Your best bet is to start breeding senior technical staff within the organization as well as continue your external search efforts—see Chapter 8 for more details.

Q3. How do we improve communications both within IT and with our internal customers because our communication flow is worse than ever before?

There's only one way to improve communications and it's not by having more staff meetings, team picnics, or quarterly get-togethers. The only way to improve communications between your end users and IT, and within IT, is via a process that we discuss in Chapter 8.

Q4. What is the secret to implementing the proper organization structure to best support your infrastructure?

The key is structuring the organization into two areas—mission critical and everything else. We've said this before. When you say the words "mission critical" in IT, most IT people think about mainframe computing because the support paradigm for mission-critical systems was second to none. Hey, they didn't focus on the technology like IT is doing today, they were simply focusing on mission critical. The secret formula to success is just that! See Chapter 8 for the details.

Q5. How do you justify everyone's roles and responsibilities in a network world?

Job descriptions alone are not enough. Everyone's roles and responsibilities need to be clearly identified via the CSPA process for each and every application. See Chapter 8 in our book *Managing the New Enterprise*.

Q6. Can we cross-train and succeed?

Yes you can!

Cross training is one of the best ways to keep staff and to ensure that you have internal knowledge in the event that one of your team members leaves the department.

Q7. Does selective outsourcing work?

Yes it does! Selective outsourcing may be one of your best tools. There are areas of the operation that we have no problem outsourcing. A good example is off-site disaster recovery data storage. But what about project management? Most organizations would never outsource project management. The truth is that most in-house technical staff people are poor project managers and they may be too closely tied to the customer. This might be a perfect place for selective outsourcing.

Q8. When do technology big guns hurt the organization?

Big guns hurt the organization when they start imposing their desires on what is truly right for the organization. It is very important to use technology-rich consultants for your business needs, not theirs.

Q9. How do we work with members of the IT organization that are not willing to change as we need to change?

The best way to deal with them is to be up front. Discuss the issues that seem to be of issue and explain that the organization is moving in this direction and that the employee is a critical part of the new environment. If they refuse to change, then it is management's job to manage.

Q10. Will all the changes ever stop?

No. The rapid pace of information technology change is strong and will continue. The imbalance between the availability of technical skills and the demand for technical skills will continue for many years to come. Change is here to stay.

Process

Q1. Our shop has no processes to help manage our mission-critical environment. We simply do not have the time and resources to do this, so which ones are the bare minimum?

That's an easy one. After years of research, the bare minimum for supporting mission-critical systems are these processes:

- Change control

- Problem management
- Client/server production acceptance

You need all three. These are the minimum requirements for building a world-class infrastructure. See Chapter 6.

Q2. Do we still need service level agreements?

Without a doubt—there needs to be external service level agreements established with your customers and internal service levels within IT between Applications Development and Production Support. Client/server computing has made communication worse than ever before. Establishing service levels are more critical than ever before! See Chapter 5 for more details.

Q3. We know the importance of metrics and how critical they are to have, but we just don't have the time to invest. What would you suggest? Which metric is the most critical to start out with?

Find a very simple method of measuring customer satisfaction. Customer satisfaction should be measured each and every time a user calls the help desk with a request for service. Don't bother sending out monthly or quarterly surveys. This old method of measuring customer satisfaction is very ineffective. Reengineer a new process. This will set you off in the right direction. It will tell you which areas need to be addressed immediately. See Chapter 2 for more details.

Q4. Should we establish a separate organization to implement metrics?

No this should be the responsibility of each manager in his or her respective area.

Q5. Should personnel involved in infrastructure activities be concerned with the processes that take customer requests

and address these requests?

Yes. How the requests are prioritized and addressed significantly influences the layering of technologies and the performance of the infrastructure.

Q6. Can I manage client/server and host-based applications using the same processes?

Yes. Many IT departments resort to different change-management processes for the single-tiered versus *n*-tier application software. The same promotion process should be used to ensure that the IT organization functions as one.

Q7. How do we manage all these desktops?

Desktop management is a very difficult job. Even with the growth of Web-based systems, basic desktop software is here to stay for a long time. We recommend that you look at software distribution utilities. You may find that the cost of the software is less than the cost of people power to keep all that software current and the asset recorded.

Q8. What about using a centralized project management tool?

One of the major problems that we found was that the IT personnel were overscheduled. Projects fail due to poor project management because resources are scheduled but aren't available when they are needed. Implementing a department-wide, project management tool is labor intensive, but the returns can be spectacular.

Q9. How do we schedule staff on multiple projects and support activities?

We again recommend that you look at a comprehensive project management tool that permits personnel resource scheduling across multiple projects. This way the employee can see what projects they are assigned to and the project manager can see who is assigned to the project. It really does work!

Q10. Do we need a career path for our staff or will the market take care of that?

Just because the supply and demand for information technology skills is not in balance, the market will not cultivate your in-house personnel. We strongly recommend that you clearly establish an employee's career and the training and skills development that will be required to move ahead. Of course, this is all tied to the overall performance of the company and IT department.

Technology

Q1. You rarely talk about technology. Is it not important?

Technology is great. It can do wonders for the business, for IT, etc. But it is the least-difficult aspect with which to deal when designing the proper infrastructure. People and process issues are making a mockery of IT.

Q2. Our shop has purchased all this nifty technology, yet we are still having a difficult time maintaining RAS. What else are we missing?

Many executives think that technology is their savior. They gobble it up and spend millions in the process. What they're missing is the proper organization structure and key processes.

Q3. This new age of computing with technology is evolving so quickly. Is it really very complex?

This new world is very complex, yet very exciting. Unfortunately, complexity plays havoc with RAS. It's fine when all this sophistication works as it's supposed to, but sometimes it doesn't work that way. We were at a company one day that had redundancy built into the hardware in case of a failure. Memory crashed on one CPU—so we put in a command to switch over to the redundant system, which it did, while repairs were made to the damaged system. After repairing the damaged system, the customer switched back to the regular system and the database was confused and corrupted.

Q4. Why does client server computing seem so complex?

The problem is that we are so accustomed to all of the applications executing on the same piece of hardware, that picturing it as a series of many computers is abstract. If you started on mainframes, the best way to envision it is to think of the PCs as one large system. Don't think of them as separate computers.

Q5. Should we go with two-tier or three-tier technology?

You may not have a choice. If you are buying off-the-shelf software, you will get what the vendor has developed. The better way to go is three-tier. It is more complex, but allows for linear growth and the option to change part of the system. Of course, once you use one vendor's middleware, you are pretty much locked in.

Q6. Do we need to standardize on one DBMS?

No. Standardize on SQL and relational DBMS technology. Buy the cheapest product that meets your business requirements.

Q7. Is the mainframe dead?

No. We recommend that you change the presentation and process layers if business changes dictate. Otherwise, most of the mainframes we've seen are state of the art technology. Remember the software is legacy, not the hardware.

Q8. What is middleware?

Middleware is software that permits the transfer of data from one software layer to another. When we want to transfer data from the presentation layer to the process layer, middleware handles this data transfer.

Q9. *Do multiple protocol networks really work?*

Yes. Multiple stacks on a desktop are a real solution to the migration from older to newer technologies. The only real problem is the move to network computing where all devices are connected to the network first and access servers second. Sometimes this is a difficult concept.

Infrastructure Assessment Program

The Industry Problem

Most IT organizations struggle with the implementation and support of client/server technology. They focus on developing and deploying applications as quickly as possible, not to mention buying up system management tools. Very little emphasis is placed on people and process issues for the network, data center, and desktop. This lack of attention for dealing with people and process issues is the largest problem in the Enterprise today.

People and process issues within IT have been around for decades but it was pretty much contained in one glass house environment. Unless organizations address these issues, networked computing will not flourish and that's putting it mildly. To elaborate on people and process issues:

People Issues

- Organizational structure
- Transitioning/mentoring staff
- Training
- Cultural differences between legacy and client/server staff
- Communication within IT and external to IT
- HR issues during the transition
- Career/skills development
- Roles and responsibilities
- Recruiting/retaining staff

Process Issues

- Disciplines (change control, problem management, etc.)
- Metrics
- Marketing and selling IT services
- Benchmarking services
- Service levels

Technology Issues

- Architecture
- Standards
- System management tools
- Integration
- Middleware
- Development tools

The Program

One to two days of onsite consulting to:

- Analyze and understand the current environment
- Acquire buy-in at senior executive level
- Gain senior level IT management commitment
- Provide a list of prioritized recommendations
- Provide a high-level road-map

The report will then take about a month to compile. Once the draft is ready, we meet with our sponsor to make sure we are on the right path. Once we agree that the report is ready we (customer, CIO and direct reports, his/her manager, and systems engineering) will meet to present our findings and get buy-in, then move forward.

Customer Requirements

1. Ability to have a one-hour meeting with executive management to establish a relationship, discusses the program, and acquire initial buy-in.

2. Ability to meet for 30 minutes separately with mid-level management from Operations, Applications Development, Help Desk, Networking, Database Administration, System Administration, etc.

3. Ability to meet for 30 minutes separately with two technical people from Systems Administration, a mainframe systems programmer (if applicable), a DBA, a help desk person, a desktop support person, and anyone else that might provide good insight into the issues.

4. If at all possible, we would like to meet with two customers for 30 minutes each.

The Deliverable

The customer receives a detailed report outlining infrastructure-related issues with associated recommendations and, just as important, buy-in at the executive level to move forward with one road-map.

The Cost

Our usual fee is $25,000.00. This includes one to two days of onsite consulting, five days to write the report, and all travel related expenses.

Service Level Agreements

Information Systems Services Cost Options Definitions

Enterprise Costs

Enterprise costs are fixed costs to sustain general operations. These charges provide for the support of connectivity, operation, and maintenance of the organization's enterprise network.

Enterprise servers provide services to more that one customer. Enterprise servers are those servers registered as of the fiscal year when the budget is approved. Servers not registered are defined as departmental servers and their support is billable at the standard professional services rate.

New equipment purchases planned for the next fiscal cycle will need to be projected on the SLA. This will provide information-systems services with information for staffing. New equipment that is not presented in the SLA will be charged a professional services fee to cover all cabling, hardware, software, and installation costs. In addition, a one-percent, per-month charge for the value of equipment to cover the cost of nonbudgeted resources will be assessed.

Professional Services

Professional services costs are charges that are incurred for services provided by information-systems services such as application services, training, desktop support, etc. Information-systems services charges a competitive cost recovery rate which is approved annually by the information systems services governance board.

```
            Service Level Agreement
                    *DATE*
               *Customer Name*


            Information Systems Services
             {Your Organization's Name}
            {Your Organization's Address}


        INFORMATION SYSTEMS SERVICES FOR
                *CUSTOMER NAME*
             FISCAL YEAR ccyy/ccyy
```

This Agreement made as of the First day of **Fiscal Year**, by and among **{organization's name}** the Information Systems Services Board **(if applicable)**, and ***CUSTOMER NAME***.

Whereas the **{organization's name}** has directed the Information Systems Services department to establish written Agreements with each Customer in order to better define the relationships between the IS function and each of its Customers,

Therefore the parties mutually agree to the following:

1. The information systems services to be provided to the Customer and respective obligations of the parties shall be in accordance with the terms of the this Service Level Agreement for Customers thereto dated for fiscal years which has been prepared specifically for this Customer and which are incorporated herein.

2. This agreement shall be in effect for the one-year period beginning on the first day of the fiscal year **{put date here}** and end on the last day of the fiscal year **(put date here}.** The Customer may terminate this Agreement upon nine months written notice to the Information Systems Services Board.

3. Changes to this Agreement can be made by written Amendment signed by all parties.

4.   The parties agree to conduct negotiations for a successor agreement for the following fiscal year in sufficient time to meet the **{organization's name}** and Customer budgeting schedules.

5.   The Customer will appoint a representative to act as the contact for the Customer. An individual performing this function will collaborate with information-systems service representatives to ensure the success of all projects. The representative does not need to have an information-systems background. It is imperative that the individual has extensive knowledge of the customer's information needs and business practices. The representative will be the primary liaison with the information-systems services contact. The representative will maintain a list of critical applications and prioritize other applications for service by the information systems services department.

6.   All Customer hardware and software interfacing with the organization's enterprise network shall be compatible with the system and operating standards established for the organization wide network. Software, database management, and operating systems installed on servers owned by the customer must be kept at the version levels specified by the information systems services department.

7.   The Customer will pay the information-systems services department in two budget cost categories: Enterprise and Professional Services for a total sum of **$ *ANNUAL BUDGET***.   These costs are: a. Enterprise Services cost for the amount of $ ***ENTERPRISE BUDGET***. Payments shall be due and made monthly in twelve equal installments of **$ * 1/12 of ENTERPRISE BUDGET***. b. The Professional Services cost for the amount of **$ *PROFESSIONAL BUDGET***. Payments shall be due and made monthly for services rendered. Interest charges incurred by information systems services department to fund its operation as a result of delinquent Customer payments will be billed directly to the Customer.

This Agreement shall become effective, as of the date written above upon execution by all of the parties.

ATTEST: {organization's name}

 BY:

By:Information Systems Services Board Chairman

I.   **Purpose**

The purpose of this SLA is to define the services provided to the Customer by the Information Systems Services Department (ISSD). These services are provided at the rates approved by the ISS Board (ISSB).

II. **Customer Service Requests**

ISSD uses a Customer Service Request (CSR) system to manage requests for services from its customers. This is an automated system available through the Enterprise network.

ISSD customers enter all requests for services into the CSR tracking system. Once entered, a production date and project schedule are negotiated between the Customer and ISSD.

III. Status Reporting

Project status is communicated through ISSD representative. This occurs through meetings, phone conversations, memorandums, E-mail, etc. On a monthly basis, the ISSD provides management reports to assist in tracking project activity. These reports detail both activity status and their associated costs.

IV. Help Desk

ISSD Help Desk services is the first line customer support for the reporting of hardware and software problems. Problems are recorded in a problem and change Control system to facilitate problem resolution. The Help Desk phone number is **{phone number}**.

Help Desk Escalation and Notification Matrix

Severity Level

1.   Failure of server/router/cabling that effects more that one department.

     Response:
          Immediate
          60 minutes - first escalation
          4 hours   - second escalation

2.   Failure of server/hub/cabling/that effects entire department of more than three customers.

     Response:
          Immediate
          2 hours - first escalation
          8 hours - second escalation

3.   Failure of PC/cable segments that effects three users of less.

     Response:
          Immediate
          24 hours - first escalation
          48 hours - second escalation

4.   Non-Priority issues.

     Response:
          Immediate
          7 days   - first escalation

V.   Services

ISSD offers a complete range of information system services. These services are customer business driven and are matched to the appropriate technology. Listed below are some of the Enterprise and Professional Services offered by ISSD.

Enterprise Services

Enterprise Services encompass the enterprise network, servers and services.

    Examples:

    Documents on demand (one time setup charge)

    Production application processing

    Problem and change management

    Business recovery services

    Enterprise printing

    Price agreement checking

    Printing and post processing services

    Purchase requisition reviews

    Public data access

    Microfilm / Microfiche

    Network software license registration

    Network software distribution

    Enterprise On-line data storage

    upport for electronic mail

    Report distribution bundling

    System performance

    System monitoring

    Security

    Integration into the enterprise network

    Wide area network performance monitoring and tuning

    Internet access

    (Add your services)

Professional Services

Professional Services costs are charges that are incurred for services provided by ISS over and above the Enterprise services. Services may be selected from the following:

    Examples:

    Project management

    Planning, research, and technical review services

    Enterprise modeling

    Strategic planning

    Business analysis

    Software recommendation

    Requests for proposal (RFP)

    Systems analysis, design and development

    Implementation of purchase/package software

    Software training

    Off-site data storage

    Installation and support of office automation services

    Application development

    Application maintenance after warranty period expires

    Form design and maintenance

    Server installation and administrative support (non Enterprise)

    System and network analysis, capacity and performance planning

Installation of direct or remote devices
Document imaging
Unplanned integration into the enterprise network
Internet web page design and integration
(add your services)

VI. Professional Services
Based on a Professional Services annual budget of $XXXXXX.XX; billing for these allocated ISSD resources is monthly on an "as consumed" basis.

VII. Software Portfolio
The ISSD will provide the Customer with an inventory of current applications that are supported. Support for applications that are not on the currently supported inventory will be negotiated. The Customer's representative will identify any maintenance needs, upgrades, and re-engineering for these applications to be included in the budget for the fiscal year.

VIII. Inventory List
The ISSD will utilize an inventory list of terminals, PCs and peripherals provided by the Asset Management System.

IX. Servers
Servers that are attached to the enterprise network will be maintained at the same software version levels specified by the ISSD. Database software must be maintained at the appropriate level to be compatible with the Enterprise network. A system management plan will be established to identify the system manager and the database administrator responsibilities, for each server. It will be the responsibility of the information manager to prepare the plan for servers that are controlled by the customer.

X. Millennium
Any applications that are not scheduled for completion of migration by **1998** will need to be reviewed for two digit year and algorithm issues occurring due to the change of century. Each customer will allocate the needed budget dollars to complete **{some percentage}** of the required year 2000 changes during fiscal cycle.

XIII. Training
The ISSD publishes a list of training courses that are offered by Customer Services. The customer will need to identify their training needs for the fiscal year.

XIV. Performance Measurements
Customer Service Request (CSR) completion dates will be negotiated among the Customer's representative and the ISSD contact. Once the

completion date is established, the staff member performing the work will be responsible for completing the work. In the event that circumstances beyond the control of the employee or ISSD result in a delay, the staff member and the ISSD contact will meet and discuss the situation with the customer. The ISSD will maintain an appropriate level of response and system up time for the enterprise network. Performance will be measured against industry standards. Additional performance measures requested by a customer will be submitted to the ISSB for review and approval.

XV. Projected Purchase of PCs, Printers etc.

The customer will provide a projection of new hardware and software. Anything in addition to this list will be subject to additional costs for installation service and support.

XVI. Projected Requirements for Network Connectivity.

The customer will identify in their SLA any new locations that will need to be connected to the Enterprise network. New equipment that is not presented in the SLA will be charged a professional services fee to cover all cabling, hardware, software, and installation costs. In addition, a 1% per month charge for the value of new equipment to cover the cost of non-budgeted resources will be assessed.

XVII. Products Supported by ISS

ISS publishes a list of products supported and services offered as part of the Enterprise network.

ISS Service Level Agreement

Fiscal Year CCYY - CCYY

XVIII. Professional Services Options (attachment)

Customer: *Customer Name*

The following attachment provides a list of planned activities for the upcoming fiscal year. It is intended that the ISSD take action on these projects during the year and in the time frames specified for each project. Customer projects noted below will be initiated as directed by the customer representative with available funding and available ISSD resources.

Planned Activity Development:

List activities for the fiscal year.

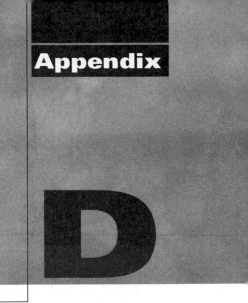

Internal Support Agreement

One of the most important, critical pieces of this puzzle was to put together a Service Level Agreement (SLA) internally between the centralized IT production support staff and the de-centralized development staff. expectations were clearly outlined for both groups.

Below are some of the key categories documented in the ISA.

Root Authority

Root access will be given to Mr. A and Ms. B to support servers AD0001 and AD0002. Mr. A and Ms. B are to support/backup each other (i.e., illness/vacation). If they're both unavailable contact Technical Support (within the data center). All changes to root will be audited to provide a trace of activity from the root user. The following activities are to be done by Technical Support upon request:

- Kernel changes
- Disk reconfigurations
- Modifying the root user environment
- Installation of any binary into the system directory structure
- Modification to any network related configuration files

- The manipulation/modification of any system daemon that is run as root
- Changes to the /etc/rc* files

The following activities (but not limited to) may be done by the applications development root owners:

- Change /etc/exports for mount directories
- Change /etc/fstab
- Add users/groups

Server Availability Hours

- 00:00 - 23:59 M, T, W, Th, and Sun
- 00:00 - 23:00 F
- 03:01 - 23:59 Sat
- 20:00 - 23:59 (Once a month for system maintenance/upgrade/testing, all will be posted through change control.)

Backups

- Full system backups start at 23:00 every Friday; total downtime is 4 hours.
- Incremental backups start at 20:00 (approximately 30 minutes Monday through Thursday).

Support Responsibility

- Technical Support: TS
- Desktop Support: DS
- Application Development: AD

Table D–1 Support, reponsibility, hours of service.

Services	Group	Types of Services	Hours
Systems Software	TS	Solaris, Sybase, installation, upgrade, maintenance.	00:00- 23:59
Systems Hardware	DS	Server, monitor, workstation, installation, maintenance.	00:00- 23:59
Application	A/D	Setup application, demos, project files access.	08:00- 18:00

Function of Each Server

Server: AD0001

This server will be the primary development machine to carry the more CPU intensive workload. Free temporary disk space is available on this machine via Unix automount. Disk quota will be set up for each project. Disk space availability will be determined by the scope of the project.

- Solaris X.X
- DNS and NIS slave server host name, IP address, aliases
- Data base server; for example: /home/sybase
- free hog disk space via automount; for example: /home/common

Server: AD0002

This machine will be used as the pre-production server.

- Solaris X.X
- Project files, data, databases; for example: /home/hrproj
- Clients personal files; for example: /home/username

Special Requests

These are different categories of special requests and their estimated completion times. These changes include investigating whether the proposed change affects other applications on the server. Technical Support will notify the requestor if the request takes longer than the estimated completion time.

Table D–2 Special Requests Estimate Completion Time

Emergency backups and restore	Processed within 4 hours.
File maintenance.	Processed within 8 hours.
Change/etc/experts for mount directories.	
Change/etc/fstab.	
Add users/group.	
Modifications to fstab, group, add user, permission change.	
Operation request.	Up to X working days.
Backup and restore for Unix files only.	
Solaris kernel.	Up to 5 working days for software that requires kernel modification.
Database change.	Up to 5 working days .
Hardware configuring.	Up to 5 working days.

With the Internal Support Agreement in place between both organizations there were less heartaches and finger pointing.

E

Marketing Materials for an Internal Audience

This material is used by Palm Beach County, Florida Information Systems Services organization for marketing to departmental customers to ensure they are aware of the scope and quality of IT services. They also publish this information in an Information Technology Survey brochure describing its services. This survey has been provided to most of the employees of the County who use IT. The survey expresses a welcome tone to the user community to be comfortable with the IT organization.

Enterprise Center

The IS Enterprise Center is a state-of-the-art automated operations center for around-the-clock processing of data and reports needed for your business operations. Our enterprise data operations are behind closed doors with the highest security system to protect the county's valuable equipment and data storage under all circumstances.

Systems Management

To efficiently support your processing workloads, IS focuses on your business-driven technologies for both the legacy and client/server environments. We are changing to add value by incorporating many technologies and deployment styles.

Quality Assurance

The IS Enterprise Center functions to initiate and maintain programs that provide a high level of computer availability with high-quality production jobs for you, our customer. The scheduling and production of accurate and timely data and reports is accomplished by control standards for all processes, procedures, and equipment.

Through a continuous-improvement quality-assurance program, our services are designed to ensure that we meet your expectations. With our business processes, our efforts are focused on availability, security, recoverability, stability, predictability, and scalability. Your changing operational demands are primary in directing us to provide the quality performance levels to meet your business needs.

Customized reports

The Enterprise Center has customized reports for each customer's needs, which can be either manually printed or electronically routed to a person at your location. The ability to dynamically create electronic versions gives you the flexibility to get reports as needed and can be more economical with reduced paper costs.

Data storage

Information data is considered one of the enterprises most valued assets. The IS Enterprise Center manages this data as a primary and most important priority, in both your daily operations or in case of a disaster.

Mission

The mission of the Enterprise Center is to be a dynamic and progressive, state-of-the-art information provider. Our investment in automation propels us to new levels of ability and achievement with our customer to become the preferred information provider.

Enterprise Center Tours

If you are interested in a tour of our facility, please call your agency consultant to arrange your request. IS can demonstrate to you those products that support your business operations.

High-Tech Equipment

The storage of data has made with efficient equipment, software, and a specially trained staff that is available 24 hours a day.

High-tech equipment that automates these processes, such as our robotics tape library, improve the efficiency of the operations process of backing up your critical information. These tapes are sent off-site in a secured vault for the highest protection standards and procedures.

Our Enterprise Center is a computing environment that includes the latest servers from various vendors, such as IBM and Sun, support the diverse software, processes, and procedures for the diverse needs of our many government customers.

Information Technology Survey

Imagine the convenience of having a comprehensive document detailing your current information systems environment. Having this valuable information available assists you in managing hardware, software, and personnel issues.

IS invites you to participate in a unique service that provides management and staff with the right information at the right time.

The service, "Information Technology Survey," is available now at all Palm Beach County agencies and departments. Highlights of the Information Technology Survey include:

- Client information review
- Transport and presentation review
- Applications review
- Staff review

Combined with a comprehensive project management control utility built into the service, IS will perform the service in an expedient and professional manner, with as little interruption as possible to your management and staff personnel. Use this information in strategic planning, problem determination, network design, desktop management, resource planning, and many more ways that are valuable. When it comes to managing networks, you need accurate reliable data, not opinions and estimates. Contact your IS agency consultant at xxx-xxxx to obtain a complete overview of this valuable service offering.

Consulting Services

A Trusting Relationship

It is the basic ingredient for a successful business partnership. At IS, we know that and prove ourselves to you every day. We need to understand your business, where you are going and help you plan how to get there.

You need a strong technical advisor, someone who understands how information system technology can make your agency succeed.

That is what IS Consulting Services is all about. Our agency consultants are there with you to help define requirements based on your business needs, formulate a solution and lead you through a successful implementation.

Strategic Vision

When it comes to developing a strategic vision for your information systems, you are putting the future of your agency or department on the line. It is imperative that you have expert counsel.

Alignment of you information systems plan with your business strategies is essential. Maximizing the return on your current information technology investment is a requirement.

IS Consulting Services is uniquely positioned to advise you on today's technology and to help you plan for your future systems and applications.

Requirements

Within IS, our expertise ranges from project management to software installation from application and database design through development and delivery.

You benefit from that experience every time you rely on us. IS stands by you every step of the way. Whether you want us to do the entire job or just supplement your staff, you can count on us for quality results.

With IS on your team, you can concentrate on your team, you can concentrate on your business objectives while we assume much of the risk for your projects.

We will deliver totally integrated systems, ensuring that deadlines are met and budgets are adhered to. Fewer risks and less hassle for you, our valued clients.

Shared vision

IS Consulting Services, in concert with the agency information officer can tailor a solution that's just right for you. We have the skills, resources, and experience to deliver precisely what you are looking for. For more information please contact IS Consulting Services at xxx-xxxx.

The IT Survey Brochure

High Tech Equipment

The storage of data has been made more efficient equipment, software and a specially trained staff that is available twenty four hours a day.

High tech equipment which automates processes, such as our robotics tape library have improved the efficiency of the operations process of backing up your critical information. These tapes are sent off-site in a secured vault for the highest protection standards and procedures.

Our Enterprise Center is a computing environment that includes the latest servers from various vendors, such as IBM and Sun Systems, support the diverse software and , processes, procedures for the diverse needs of our many governmental customers.

Mission

The mission of the Enterprise Center is to be a dynamic and progressive state of the art information provider. Our investment in automation propels us to new levels of ability and achievement with our customer to become the preferred information provider.

Enterprise Center Tours

If you are interested in a tour of our facility, please call your Agency consultant to arrange your request. ISS can demonstrate to you those products that support your business operations

12/98

ISS Enterprise Center

Serving Your Business Needs

**Information Systems Services
Palm Beach County, Florida**

Enterprise Center

The ISS Enterprise Center is a state-of-the-art automated operations center for round-the-clock processing of data and reports needed for your business operations. Our enterprise data operations are behind closed doors with the highest security system to protect the county's valuable equipment and data storage under all circumstances.

System Management

To efficiently maintain support for your existing processing workloads, ISS is focused on your business-driven technologies for both the legacy and client server environments. We are changing to add value by incorporating many technologies and deployment styles.

Quality Assurance

The ISS Enterprise Center functions to initiate and maintain programs that provide a high level of computer availability with high quality production jobs for you, our customer. The scheduling and production of accurate and timely data and reports is accomplished by control standards for all processes, procedures and equipment.

Through a continuous improvement quality assurance program, our services are designed to insure that we meet your expectations. With our business processes our efforts are focused on availability, security, recoverability, stability, predictability, and scalability. Your changing operational demands are primary in directing us to provide the quality performance levels to meet your business needs.

Customized Reports

The Enterprise Center has customized reports for each customer's needs, which can be either manually printed or electronically routed to a printer at your location. The ability to dynamically create electronic forms gives you the flexibility to create reports as needed and can be more economical with reduced paper costs.

Data Storage

Information data is considered one the enterprise's most valuable asset. The ISS Enterprise Center manages this data as a primary and most important priority, in both your daily operations or in the event of a disaster.

**Information
Systems
Services**

ISS Business Process

Palm Beach County's Information Systems Services (ISS) has developed, tested, and is implementing a new comprehensive approach to Process and Project Management. This unique, systematic procedure assures the delivery of superior products and services.

The emphasis of our ISS Business Process is on customer participation and customer satisfaction. Utilization of this innovative methodology will provide quality products and services that are *predictable, repeatable,* and *measurable*.

Following a three stage management process, the methodology incorporates these essential components:

- *Concept Stage*
  High-level System Requirements Definition
  Service Quality Assessment
  Proposal Generation and Approval
  Technical Risk Analysis
  Evaluation/Assessment Process
  Project Plan Generation and Approval

- *Execute Stage*
  Establishment of Detailed Requirements
  Detailed Work Plans
  Change Management
  Acceptance Review and Approval

- *Closure Stage*
  Quality Assurance Report
  Project Summary Report
  Service Quality Assessment
  Project Closure

Working with the customer, ISS will provide superior competitive products and services that will meet or exceed customer expectations. This new approach to Process and Project Management will serve as a model for other governmental and non-commercial organizations.

ISS is providing this process innovation to address the county's operational requirements and technology demands. Our vision is the development of a quality business process, in an environment where ISS and the customer are mutual partners.

11/96

Information Technology Survey

ISS Professional Services

Information Systems Services

Imagine the convenience of having a comprehensive document detailing your current information systems environment. Having this valuable information available assists you in managing hardware, software, and personnel issues.

ISS invites you to participate in a unique service that provides management and staff with the right information at the right time. The service, "Information Technology Survey," is available now to all Palm Beach County Agencies and Departments. Highlights of the Information Technology Survey include:

- Client Information Review
- Transport and Presentation Review
- Data Facility Review
- Applications Review
- Staff Review

Combined with a comprehensive Project Management control utility, built into the service, ISS will perform the service in an expedient and professional manner, with as little interruption as possible to your management and staff personnel. Utilize this information in strategic planning, problem determination, network design, desktop management, resource planning, and many more valuable ways. When it comes to managing networks, you need accurate reliable data, not opinions and estimates. Contact your ISS Agency Consultant at 355-4496 to obtain a complete overview of this valuable service offering.

6/96

ISS Consulting Services

A trusting relationship

It's the basic ingredient for a successful business partnership. At ISS, we know that and prove ourselves to you every day. We need to understand your business, where you're going and help you plan how to get there.

You need a strong technical advisor, someone who understands how information systems technology can make your agency succeed.

That's what ISS Consulting Services is all about. Our Agency Consultants are there with you to help you define requirements based on your business needs, formulate a solution and lead you through a successful implementation.

Strategic Vision

When it comes to developing a strategic vision for your information systems, you're putting the future of your agency or department on the line. It's imperative that you have expert counsel.

Alignment of your information systems plan with your business strategies is essential. Maximizing the return on your current information technology investment is a requirement.

ISS Consulting Services is uniquely positioned to advise you on today's technology and to help you plan for your future systems and applications.

Requirements

Within ISS our expertise ranges from project management to software installation, from application and database design through development and delivery.

You benefit from that experience every time you rely on us. ISS stands by you every step of the way. Whether you want us to do the entire job or just supplement your staff, you can count on us for quality results.

With ISS on your team, you can concentrate on your business objectives while we assume much of the risk for your projects.

We will deliver totally integrated systems, ensuring that deadlines are met and budgets are adhered to. Fewer risks and less hassle for you, our valued clients.

Shared Vision

ISS Consulting Services, in concert with the Agency Information Officer can tailor a solution that's just right for you. We've got the skills, resources, and experience to deliver precisely what you're looking for. For more information please contact ISS Consulting Services at 355-4496.

Information Systems Services
Palm Beach County, Florida

Bibliography

Axelrod, R. (1984). *The Evolution of Cooperation*. New York: Basic Books.

Beck, N. (1992). *Shifting Gears: Thriving in the New Economy*. Toronto: HarperCollins.

Borthick, A Faye; Roth, Harold P. "Understanding client/server computing," *Management Accounting* (76:2), August 1994, pp.36-41.

Bridges, W. (1994). *JobShift: How to Prosper in a Workplace without Jobs*. Reading, MA: Addison-Wesley Publishing Company.

Cascio, W. (1992). *Managing Human Resources* (3rd ed.). New York: McGraw-Hill.

Davis-Blake, A., and Uzzi, B. (1993). "Determinants of employment externalization: A study of temporary workers and independent contractors," *Administrative Science Quarterly, 38*, 195-223.

DeSantis, G., Jackson, B. "Coordination of information technology management: Team-based structures and computer-based communication systems," *Journal of Management Information Systems* (10:4), 1995, pp. 85-110.

Diamond, S. "Client/server: Myths & realities," *Journal of Systems Management* (46:4), July/August 1995, pp. 44-48.

Doeringer, P., and Piore, M. (1976). *Internal Labor Markets and Manpower Analysis*. Lexington, MA: C. Heath and Company.

Donaldson, L. (1990). The ethereal hand: Organizational economics and management theory. *Academy of Management Review*, 15, 369-381.

Duchessi, P., Chengalur-Smith, I. "Client/server benefits, problems, best practices." Communications of the ACM (41:5), May 1998, pp. 87-94.

Fitzgerald, J., and Dennis, A. *Business Data Communications and Networking*, John Wiley & Sons, Inc., New York, 1996.

Galup, S., Saunders, C., Nelson, and Cerveny, R. "The Use of Virtual Staff and Managers in a Local Government Environment," *Communication Research* (24:6), December 1997, pp. 698-730.

Granovetter, M. (1974). *Getting a Job: A Study of Contacts and Careers*. Cambridge, MA: Harvard University Press.

Griesing, D. (1990). "The human side of economic organization." *Academy of Management Review*, 15, 478-499.

Hackman, J. R., and Oldham, G.R. (1980). *Work Design*. Reading, MA: Addison-Wesley Publishing Company.

Hennart, J. F. (1993). "Explaining the swollen middle: Why most transactions are a mix of 'Market' and 'Hierarchy.'" *Organization Science*, 4, 529-547.

Kanungo, R.N. (1982). "The measurement of job and work involvement." *Journal of Applied Psychology*, 67, 341-349.

Krackhardt, D., and Kilduff, M. (1990). "Friendship patterns and culture: The control of organizational diversity." *American Anthropologist*, 92, 142-164.

Krackhardt, D., and Porter, L. (1985). "When friends leave: A structural analysis of the relationship between turnover and stayers' attitudes." *Administrative Science Quarterly*, 30, 2424-261.

Krackhardt, D., and Porter, L. (1986). "The Snowball Effect: Turnover embedded in communication networks." *Journal of Applied Psychology*, 71(1), 50-55.

Krackhardt, D., and Stern, R.N. (1988). "Informal networks and organizational crises: An experimental simulation." *Social Psychological Quarterly*, 51, 123-140.

Kern, H., and Johnson, R. (1994). *Rightsizing the New Enterprise: The Proof, Not the Hype*, Sun Microsystems Press—Prentice Hall, California.

Kern, H., Johnson, R., Hawkins, M, Lyke,H., Kennedy, W., and Cappel, M. (1995). *Networking The New Enterpise: The Proof, Not the Hype*, Sun Microsystems Press—Prentice Hall, California.

Kern, H., Johnson, R., Hawkins, M., and Law, A. (1996). *Managing the New Enterprise: The Proof Not the Hype*, Sun Microsystems Press—Prentice Hall, California.

Kern, H., Johnson, R., Galup, S., and Horgan, D. (1998). *Building the New Enterprise: People, Processes, and Technology*, Sun Microsystems Press—Prentice Hall, California.

King, Julia "Mainframers win ticket to ride client/server bus," *Computerworld* (28:30), July 8, 1996, pp.1 and 16.

Kliem, R. "Managing the People side of client/server architecture," *Journal of Systems Management* (47:1), January/February 1996, pp.24-28.

Lindberg, L.N., Campbell, J.C., and Hollingsworth, J.R. (1991). "Economic governance and the analysis of structural change in the American economy."

In J.C. Campbell, J.R. Hollingsworth, & L.N. Lindberg (Eds.), *Governance of the American Economy*, New York: Cambridge University Press.

Lee, Denis M S; Trauth, E.M; Farwell, D. "Critical skills and knowledge requirements of IS professionals: A joint academic/industry investment," *MIS Quarterly* (19:3), September 1995, pp. 313-340.

Magnum, G., Mayall, D., and Nelson, K. (1985). "The temporary help industry: A response to the dual internal labor market." *Industrial Labor Relations Review, 38, 599-611.*

Mahoney, J.T. (1992). "The choice of organizational form: Vertical financial ownership versus other methods of vertical integration." *Strategic Management Journal*, 13, 559-584.

Martin, Richard J. "In praise of old dogs," *Journal of Systems Management* (45:12), December 1994, pp.57-59.

Merton, R.K. (1968). *Social Theory and Social Structure* (Enlarged Edition). New York: Free Press.

Nelson, R.E. (1986). Social networks and organizational intervention: Insights from an area-wide labor-management committee. *Journal of Applied Behavioral Science,*22, 65-76.

Nelson, R. E. (1989). The strength of strong ties: Social networks and inter-group conflict in organizations. *Academy of Management Journal*, 32, 377-401.

Nelson, R.E., and Mathews, K.M. (1991). "Social networks of high performing organizations." *Journal of Business Communication*, 28, 367-386.

Nelson, R.E., and Mathews, K.M. (1991). "The use of cause maps and social network analysis in organizational diagnosis." *Journal of Applied Behavioral Science*, 27, 379-397.

Ouchi, W. (1979). "A conceptual framework for the design of organizational control mechanisms." *Management Science, 25, 833-848.*

Palm Beach County Technology Transformation Plan, April 10, 1995.

Perrow, C. (1986). *Complex Organizations: A Critical Essay* (3rd ed.). McGraw-Hill, Inc: New York, NY.

Powell, W. (1990). "Neither market nor hierarchy: Network forms of organization." In Barry Staw and L.L. Cummings (Eds.) *Research in Organization Behavior: Vol. 12*, pp. 295-336. Greenwich, CT: JAI Press.

Provan, K. (1993). "Embeddedness, interdependence, and opportunism in organizational supplier-buyer networks." *Journal of Management*, 19, 841-856.

Saunders, C., Hu, Q., and Gebelt, M. (1997). "Achieving success in information systems outsourcing." *California Management Review*, 39 (2), 63-79.

Schulte, R., "Middleware and Three-Tier Architectures" GartnerGroup Symposium/Itxpo 95: Managing the Revolution, October 9-13, 1995, Day 5.

Sims, H.P., Szilagyi, A.D., & Keller, R.T. (1976). "The measurement of job characteristics." *Academy of Management Journal*, 19, 195-212.

Uzzi, B. (1997). "Social structure and competition in interfirm networks: The paradox of embeddedness." *Administrative Science Quarterly*, 42, 35-67.

Walker, G., and Weber, D. (1984). A transaction cost approach to make-or-buy decisions. *Administrative Science Quarterly*, 29, 373-391.

Williamson, O. (1981). "The economics of organization: The transaction cost approach." *American Journal of Sociology*, 87, 548-577.

Weston, R. "Client/server evolution: Thin clients, fat servers," *Computerworld* (32:6), February 9, 1998, p. 20.

Index

reliability, availability, and serviceability xi, 21, 35, 38

retaining staff 20

Rightsizing The New Enterprise 17, 76, 77, 78, 119, 144

roles and responsibilities 19, 147

S

SAP 115

scheduling 20

security 19, 51

server consolidation 19

service agreement 86

service level agreements 20, 149

services 162

skills development 19

software 19

Software Development (Building Reliable Systems) 76

software distribution 19

SQL 152

standards 20

status reporting 162

storage management 20

Sun Microsystems 38, 85, 141

supply chain management 141

Sybase 95

system administration 25, 144

system management 25, 29, 79

system management tools 20

systems administration 128

systems programmers 54

systems programming 57

T

tape librarian 28, 61, 64

technology 151, 156

Training 19

training 135, 164

transitional staff 19

TSO 53

U

UniCenter 37

Unix 21, 54, 65, 67

V

version/release management 20

VTAM 53

W

Wal-Mart 141

worldclass infrastructure 141